EARLY MUSIC SERIES 15

THE EARLY FL

EARLY MUSIC SERIES

THE EARLY FLUTE

BY

JOHN SOLUM

with a chapter on the Renaissance flute
by
ANNE SMITH

CLARENDON PRESS · OXFORD

Oxford University Press, Walton Street, Oxford OX2 6DP
Oxford New York
Athens Auckland Bangkok Bombay
Calcutta Cape Town Dar es Salaam Delhi
Florence Hong Kong Istanbul Karachi
Kuala Lumpur Madras Madrid Melbourne
Mexico City Nairobi Paris Singapore
Taipei Tokyo Toronto
and associated companies in
Berlin Ibadan

Oxford is a trade mark of Oxford University Press

Published in the United States
by Oxford University Press Inc., New York

All except Chapter 2 © John Solum 1992
Chapter 2 © Anne Smith 1992

First published 1992
Paperback edition 1995

British Library Cataloguing in Publication Data
Data available

Library of Congress Cataloging in Publication Data
Solum, John
The early flute / by John Solum; with a chapter on the
Renaissance flute by Anne Smith.—(Early music series; 15)
Includes bibliographical references and index.
1. Flute. 2. Flute music—Bibliography. I. Title.
II. Series: Early music series (London, England: 1976); 15.
ML935.S66 1995 788.3′219—dc20
ISBN 0-19-816575-7

1 3 5 7 9 10 8 6 4 2

Printed in Great Britain
on acid-free paper by
St Edmundsbury Press,
Bury St Edmunds, Suffolk

To Penny,
Eric, and Andrew

PREFACE

THIS book is conceived primarily as a guide for modern flautists who are interested in entering the realm of early-music performance on period instruments, or for those who have already acquired a taste for early flutes and who wish to further their enquiry with some guidance. It is also written for players of other early-music instruments and directors of early-music ensembles who wish to find out more about the early flute.

It is not a tutor (which would deal extensively with basic tone production, breathing, posture, embouchure, articulation, and fingering). However, it is meant to encourage the playing of the early flute, or at least the development of a sympathetic understanding of the instrument. For those who wish to play, it is not a substitute for a good teacher. This book examines the early-music revival as it relates to the transverse flute and gives a history of the early flute, including a chapter on the Renaissance flute by Anne Smith covering that instrument in a nutshell. Additional chapters discuss how to acquire instruments, their care and maintenance, sources for learning about technique and style, and recommendations regarding repertoire and editions of flute music. A final chapter contains advice to the modern player and attempts to relate the early flute to the modern flute.

The scope of this book encompasses the Renaissance, baroque, and classical flute, but not the Romantic flute. The latter would certainly require a separate volume, so varied are its manifestations as an instrument, so numerous are the treatises which deal with it.

In the initial stages of planning this book, a decision was made to cite only material which was originally written in English or has been translated into English. (Several foreign-language sources are mentioned in Chapter 7, however.) English-language treatises are discussed only if they have been made available to the general reader in modern reprints or facsimile editions. Of course, readers are strongly encouraged to study foreign-language sources and, if they can be found, English-language treatises which have not yet been reprinted.

Terminology regarding the flute is sometimes confusing. Before proceeding further, some clarification must be made regarding common names which apply to the flute. Until the middle of the eighteenth century, the term 'flute' or 'flauto' meant recorder. To distinguish the recorder from the transverse flute, the latter was usually called 'flauto traverso', 'flûte traversière', 'traversa', or

'German flute'.[1] Today, we use these terms interchangeably, although 'German flute' is rarely used and 'flauto traverso' is frequently shortened to 'traverso', which is incorrect but universally accepted. In our modern discussion of flutes, we use the terms 'Renaissance flute', 'baroque flute', and 'classical flute' to refer to the transverse flutes which were in use in the Renaissance, baroque, and classical periods of music. Throughout this book, the generic term 'flute' will also sometimes be used. The term 'simple system' usually refers to wooden or ivory flutes of four to eight keys or more. In truth, such flutes do not have a system of keys (unlike clarinets, where specific systems exist, such as Albert's). However, because the term 'simple system' is universally acknowledged to mean the general type of non-metallic pre-Boehm flute with multiple keys, this book will continue to use it.

It has become common practice in recent years to refer to different parts of the traverso as 'head joint', 'upper body joint', 'lower body joint', and 'foot joint'. The eighteenth-century flautist, composer, and writer, Johann Joachim Quantz (1697–1773), used such terms as *Kopfstücke* and *Mittelstücke*, which Edward R. Reilly has translated as 'head piece' and 'middle piece'.[2] Since 'joint' also means the location at which two pieces of the instrument are joined, it is less confusing to use the term 'piece' to indicate a section of the flute. Therefore, this book will use the terms 'head piece', 'upper middle piece', 'lower middle piece', and 'foot piece' to indicate the principal sections of the four-piece flute.

Musical notes using letters rather than musical notation are indicated as follows:

CC to BB   C to B   c to b   c′ to b′   c″ to b″   c‴ to b‴

---

[1] From existing autographs of Bach's flute music, one may note that Bach used the term 'traversiere' (Ouverture in B minor, BWV 1067), 'travers.' (Sonata in B minor, BWV 1030) and 'traversa' (Sonata in A major, BWV 1032). The original engraved edition of the Sonata from the Musical Offering specifies 'Traversa'. Handel's autograph of his Sonata in E minor states 'Travers.'. Mozart's autographs contain the term 'flauto traverso' (Andante in C major, K. 315), and 'flauto' (Flute and Harp Concerto, K. 299, and the Quartet in A major for flute and strings, K. 298).

[2] Johann Joachim Quantz, *On Playing the Flute*, ed. and trans. Edward R. Reilly (London: Faber & Faber, 1966; 2nd ed., 1985), 31–2.

When describing a key or note without specific reference to an octave, the capital letter is generally used, such as 'D major' or the 'F key'.

Titles of treatises and musical works which are given in French retain the original spelling even when it may differ from modern usage.

J.S.

ACKNOWLEDGEMENTS

THIS book draws upon my nearly four decades of personal associations within the world of music, during which time I have been the recipient of much kindness, generosity, and inspiration. I thank Bruce Phillips of Oxford University Press for his guidance in many matters and to Patrick Carnegy for giving valuable suggestions in the conceptual stages of this book. At various stages of the manuscript, knowledgeable advice on matters both large and small was rendered by Howard Schott. Other helpful conversations have been with the flautists Stephen Preston, Lisa Beznosiuk, Richard Wyton, and Donald Peck, the harpsichordist Lionel Party, the violinists Stanley Ritchie and Anthony Martin, and the violin restorer, William Monical. Christoph Wolff, Robert L. Marshall, Tula Giannini, and Teri Towe helped to clarify some historical matters. The mechanics of buying musical instruments at auction were explained to me by Graham Wells, Frances Gillham, and Edward Stollar. The instrument-maker Friedrich von Huene has been very generous with his time in many ways, including the lending of photographs and drawings from his personal collection. Others who have co-operated in providing useful photographs or actually have taken photographs at my request include Marcia Brown, Robert Eliason, Robert A. Lehman, Stewart Pollens, D. Samuel Quigley, Charles Rudig, Robert Sheldon, Charles and Helen Valenza, Graham Wells, and Robert Woosnam-Savage.

The text has been greatly strengthened by comments and advice offered after being read in part by Roderick Cameron, Catherine Folkers, Friedrich von Huene, Igor Kipnis, Robert A. Lehman, Ardal Powell, Thomas Prescott, and Edward R. Reilly. I take responsibility for all the errors which remain as well as for the inadvertent omissions which inevitably will become apparent.

I especially appreciate Anne Smith's wonderful co-operation in preparing her chapter on the Renaissance flute. I also gratefully acknowledge the friendly assistance of Sabrina Weiss Pape, Sarah Ransom Canino, and Marie Imperati of the Dickinson Music Library at Vassar College, Poughkeepsie, New York, during the writing of this book. My task would have been much more difficult without their courteous help.

CONTENTS

LIST OF FIGURES

I

Some Historical Considerations

OF all the musical instruments which we call 'modern', perhaps none has changed more radically from its historical precursors than the transverse flute. To begin with, a visual comparison alone offers striking differences. The modern flute is usually made of metal and has complicated fingering mechanisms soldered to the tube. Renaissance, baroque, and classical flutes, on the other hand, are made of wood or ivory and are notable for their simplicity of design and comparative lack of mechanical devices.

For much of the first half of the twentieth century (especially in the period between the two World Wars), the old-style flute was generally considered to be a historical curiosity and a museum piece. These were the years when the Boehm-style flute achieved virtually universal acceptance by professionals. It was assumed then that the Boehm-system flute was the ultimate perfection of the instrument, embodying countless 'improvements' upon the simple instrument which had served music for over two hundred years. Typical of the prevailing attitude towards the old instruments is a statement by William Kincaid, first flute of the Philadelphia Orchestra from 1921 to 1960. Responding to a question about whether or not he ever played any of his antique flutes in public, Kincaid replied, 'No, they lack the full sonority. Besides, they are too difficult to play. You see, I would have to practice on them. Despite the limitations of these ancient instruments, the performers of the past must have managed very well with them for lots of beautiful music was written for the flute before Boehm improved the instrument.'[1]

Few people could have imagined then that the Renaissance, baroque, classical, and early Romantic flutes would ever again be played in public concerts by professionals. For one thing, the sound of the old flutes was so small; it was impractical to play them in the large concert halls which had been built for large audiences. Moreover, most old flutes were at different pitches (usually lower) from those of modern instruments. In order to play together with modern instruments, the overall length of surviving old flutes would have to be changed

---

[1] Quoted in Rafael Kammerer, 'William Kincaid: Sights Set on a New Horizon', *Musical America* (Aug. 1960), 28.

to reach modern pitch. (In fact, this happened to many old flutes.) Hardly anyone dared to dream that some day an entire orchestra would adopt the pitch of the old flutes and other surviving antique instruments of fixed pitch.

When comparing old and modern instruments, it is interesting to note that many instruments which are called 'modern' are, in fact, products of the nineteenth century. The 'modern' Steinway piano was perfected in the last half of the nineteenth century. The 'modern' flute was developed by Theobald Boehm (1794–1881) by the middle of the last century—over a hundred and forty years ago. The 'modern' symphony orchestra is a creature of the nineteenth century, its size and instrumentation having been largely determined by the requirements of works by such composers as Brahms, Wagner, Mahler, and Bruckner. When we compare early flutes with the 'modern' flute, we are really comparing flutes all of which existed before the twentieth century.

Until the twentieth century, most musical performers were generally concerned about music of their own time, rather than about music of previous generations or centuries. Thus, Bach's concerts generally involved music by himself and his contemporaries. Haydn, Mozart, and Beethoven were mostly concerned about the music of their own time, although, of course, it is known that Mozart admired the music of Bach and Handel, and Beethoven performed some of Mozart's music. Even more notably a twentieth-century idea is the concept of playing music of previous centuries on instruments which existed at the time of the composer in a style which attempts to approximate that which was known to the composer, as well as considering the aesthetic, social, and philosophical thinking of the composer's time. Such a practice is what is now called 'early music' or 'historically informed performance'.

'Authenticity'

Playing on period instruments does not guarantee authenticity. Many early-music performers avoid making claims of authenticity because they are aware of the fact that we will never know exactly what performances actually sounded like before the invention of the gramophone. One can study notation, treatises, documents, instruments, and history, but ultimately there remains much uncertainty about how performances actually sounded hundreds of years ago. Of course, then as now, subjective feeling, personal interpretation, and personality play an important part in any good performance. The power of communication is a key factor in any successful performance. It has frequently been said that it is preferable to give a vivid, expressive early-music performance on modern instruments than a dull, lifeless performance on period instruments. What historically correct instruments can do, if played in a historically informed manner, is to place us—performers and audiences—closer to the composer's own sound-world. Questions of dynamics, balance, tempo, pitch, nuance, tone colour, and articulation, which can be problematical when playing old music on modern instruments, are frequently solved simply by playing the music on historically correct instruments.

The Early Flute and the Early-Music Revival

The modern rebirth of the old-style flute did not occur as an isolated event. It has been a relatively recent development within the context of the world-wide early-music revival, resulting from many threads of enquiry and accomplishment which have been woven together over many decades. It is a complex story involving musicologists, editors, publishers, instrument-makers, instrument collectors, museum curators, dealers, librarians, professional and amateur performers, and teachers, as well as such technical matters as the invention of recorded sound and the development of inexpensive photocopying. Many aspects of this revival are discussed at length in *The Early Music Revival: A History* by Harry Haskell.[2] The traverso's reappearance has come relatively late in the revival, certainly long after the re-establishment of the recorder and the harpsichord.

In truth, the simple-system flute had never really completely died out. Such flutes have been used by Irish flute bands throughout most of the present century,[3] and there have always been some self-taught flautists—sometimes now called buskers—who have preferred simple wooden flutes with a few keys. There were a number of renowned flautists active in the last half of the nineteenth century who rejected the Boehm flute in preference to the simple-system instrument. Among these were Joachim Andersen (1847–1909), Luigi Hugues (1836–1913), Adolf Terschak (1832–1901), Franz Doppler (1821–83), Karl Doppler (1825–1900), Ernesto Koehler (1849–1907), and Maximilian Schwedler (b. 1853).[4] Georges Laurent (1886–1964), first-desk flute of the Boston Symphony Orchestra from 1921 to 1952, began his flute studies at the age of 11 on a seven-keyed wooden instrument.

The 1909 edition of François Devienne's flute method (originally published *c.*1794), revised and augmented by Philippe Gaubert, is intended for both the

---

[2] Published by Thames and Hudson, 1988. See also Thomas Binkley, 'A Perspective on Historical Performance', *Historical Performance*, 1: 1 (1988).

[3] See Derek Greer, 'The Flute Bands of Ireland', *Flutist Quarterly*, 11: 1 (1985) 42–3.

[4] See Leonardo de Lorenzo, *My Complete Story of the Flute* (New York: The Citadel Press, 1951; repr., Lubbock, Tex.: Texas Tech University Press, forthcoming), 275, 322–3. Schwedler developed a 'Reform flute', a complex instrument of 15 or so keys, which was based on the 8-keyed flute.

Boehm-system flute and the 'ancienne' or 'ordinaire' flute, meaning the eight-keyed flute. Fingering charts are included for both types, and an illustration of an eight-keyed flute accompanies these charts.[5] Maximilian Schwedler, first flute of the Leipzig Gewandhaus Orchestra, published a tutor for the old-style flute in 1899, with a second edition appearing in 1910 and a third in 1923.[6]

Simple-system flutes continued to be made by the thousands throughout the latter part of the nineteenth century and into the twentieth century in Germany, France, England, and America. Many of these instruments were of the so-called Meyer system of grenadilla or rosewood, with comparatively large embouchure holes, large tone holes, and as many as thirteen keys.

Replica baroque flutes were also made before the modern post-war early-music revival. Arnold Dolmetsch, who had begun to make replica recorders about 1920, apparently never made a replica traverso. One who did was Eugene Joseph Albert of Brussels. The Dayton C. Miller Flute Collection at the Library of Congress, Washington, DC, contains two replicas made by Albert in 1924: a boxwood and ivory replica of an original traverso by Hotteterre, *c.*1700, and an ebony and ivory two-keyed replica of an original flute by Quantz of *c.*1750.[7]

Recordings

Sound recordings are a valuable documentation of the early flute's revival by professionals in the twentieth century. With the advent of the long-playing record in the 1950s, a number of players became extremely active in the recording studios. One of the first of these was Ludwig von Pfersmann, who recorded Bach sonatas, Bach's Musical Offering, and a Vivaldi concerto with the harpsichordist, Isolde Ahlgrimm. Von Pfersmann used a nineteenth-century conical wooden Boehm-system flute with ring keys made by G. M. Bürger of Strasburg. While this is not, strictly speaking, a traverso, nevertheless these recordings were clearly a serious attempt to seek out the style and sounds of the baroque era. Gustav Scheck, who began playing the baroque flute in the 1920s,[8] made a number of pioneering traverso recordings in the 1950s using a one-keyed boxwood flute by F. G. A. Kirst (1750–1806). Scheck's recordings include the Leopold Hoffman Concerto (formerly attributed to Haydn) in 1952

---

[5] See Devienne, *Célèbre Méthode Complète de Flûte* (Paris: Alphonse Leduc, 1909).

[6] See Dayton C. Miller, *Catalogue of Books and Literary Material Relating to the Flute and Other Musical Instruments* (Cleveland, Oh.: privately printed, 1935), 103. The title of Schwedler's book is *Des Flötenspielers erster Lehrmeister.*

[7] See Laura E. Gilliam and William Lichtenwanger, *The Dayton C. Miller Flute Collection: A Checklist of the Instruments,* (Washington, DC: Library of Congress, 1961), nos. 428 and 429, and Michael Seyfrit, *Musical Instruments in the Dayton C. Miller Flute Collection at the Library of Congress: A Catalog,* i (Washington, DC: Library of Congress, 1982), nos. 126 and 127.

[8] See Eve O'Kelly, *The Recorder Today* (Cambridge: Cambridge University Press, 1990), 6.

and the Bach Ouverture in B minor in 1954. Hans-Martin Linde made a wide variety of recordings using a flute by Martin Metzler of *c.*1750, among which are the Leclair Concerto, recorded in 1956, Bach's Partita in A minor, and many works from Telemann's *Musique de Table*. Perhaps the most active of all the traverso players who became prominent in the 1950s was Leopold Stastny, a member of Nikolaus Harnoncourt's Concentus Musicus, Vienna. Using a traverso by C. A. Grenser, he recorded the Bach sonatas, Musical Offering, and Ouverture in B minor, and works by Handel, Hotteterre, Marais, Quantz, Telemann, and Vivaldi. The traverso-player in the first period-instrument recording of the Bach Brandenburg Concertos was Joseph Bopp, who recorded the Fifth Concerto in 1951 using an original traverso by Greve.[9]

Another pioneering European traverso-player was Frans Vester (1922–87) of the Netherlands. Much admired and beloved, he was a bold innovator and a ceaseless experimenter in applying historical performance practices to his musical interpretations. He was the first flautist to record the Mozart Flute Concertos on period instruments. His influence as a teacher was widespread, with students coming to him from many parts of the world. Among his most prominent students are Barthold Kuijken, Janet See, Lucius Voorhorst, Jane Bowers, Greer Ellison, Stephen Schulz, and Alain Winkelman.[10]

Two other Continental flautists who have made highly influential recordings on the traverso are Frans Brüggen and Barthold Kuijken. These two artists have now achieved an international renown reserved for the élite among early-music performers. Brüggen's brilliant career has combined his gifts as a recorder-player, baroque flautist, and conductor. Born in Amsterdam in 1934, he acquired something of Vester's unwillingness to accept routine interpretations by rethinking virtually every phrase, never taking anything for granted. He has startled his listeners with his genuinely fresh, sometimes even provocative interpretations. He has worked closely for many years with the harpsichordist Gustav Leonhardt and the cellist Anner Bylsma. In recent years he has devoted considerable time to projects with the Orchestra of the 18th Century, a period-instrument ensemble.

Many of Kuijken's activities as a performer and recording artist have been in an ensemble with his two brothers, the violinist Sigiswald and the cellist and viola-da-gamba-player, Wieland. Singly and as a group, they perform with a sensitivity and refinement which commands wide admiration. Kuijken has also

[9] See 'Baroque Flute Discography' compiled by Dale Higbee, *Early Music*, 7: 2 (1979).
[10] A *Festschrift* entitled *Concerning the Flute*, ed. Rien de Reede, was published in honour of Vester in 1984 (Amsterdam: Broekmans & Van Poppel) upon his retirement from the Royal Conservatory in The Hague. The book contains articles by Jane Bowers, Betty Bang Mather, David Lasocki, Nikolaus Delius, Mirjam Nastasi, Karl Ventzke, Karl Lenski, Rineke Smilde, and Frans Vester.

gained prominence as a teacher, attracting a large class of serious traverso-players.

Other well-known traverso-players active in Europe are Wilbert Hazelzet and Konrad Hünteler, both of whom have made outstanding recordings.

England's first internationally recognized modern master of the traverso is Stephen Preston, who began as a Boehm-system flautist but switched to historical instruments early in his career. He is a compelling performer, playing with wit and imagination. In addition to baroque and classical flute, Preston, more than any other flautist of our time, has mastered the simple-system flutes of the first half of the nineteenth century, bringing his early-music expertise well into the Romantic era of music. Ever since he withdrew from playing with the English period-instrument orchestras, such as the English Concert and the Academy of Ancient Music, much of the traverso work with these groups has been handled with skilful dexterity by Lisa Beznosiuk. Her recordings, and those of Preston, are highly regarded. Some of Preston's earliest recording activity involved the collaboration of Nicholas McGegan as co-flautist. McGegan's busy conducting career has regrettably left him with little time to perform on the traverso.

In America, one of the first professional early-music wind-players was Shelley Gruskin, who was a member of the New York Pro Musica from 1961 to 1974. He has played a variety of wind instruments, including recorder, Renaissance flute, crumhorn, rauschpfeife, bagpipe, and gemshorn. He took up the baroque flute in 1958 and, with the exception of Colin Sterne, was apparently the first American to play the baroque flute professionally.[11]

Other Aspects of the Early-Music Revival

There are other aspects of the early-music revival which have influenced the renewed interest in the playing of historical flutes. Among these are the development of musical instrument collections, reprints and translations of treatises into English, higher standards of editions of music, instrument-makers copying historical models, and the use of pitches other than A=440.

Musical Instrument Collections

The collecting of musical instruments is perhaps as old as music itself. In the world today are a large number of public collections, many of which include historic flutes. The existence of these collections has made it possible for

---

[11] See Eleanor Lawrence, 'Interview with Shelley Gruskin', *Newsletter of the National Flute Association*, 6: 3 (1981).

scholars to make systematic studies of the development of the flute and for instrument-makers to study and measure the most outstanding of these instruments for the purpose of making replicas of them. One of the first great modern collections (which is now the nucleus of the Boston Museum of Fine Arts collection) was formed by an English clergyman, Francis Galpin (1858–1945). Another important English collector was Adam Carse (1878–1958), who also carried out important research and writing on the history of musical instruments and the eighteenth-century orchestra. Among the collections which contain important examples of baroque and classical flutes are the following.

London	Victoria and Albert Museum
	Horniman Museum (incorporating the Dolmetsch Collection)
Oxford	The Bate Collection of Historical Instruments at the Faculty of Music, University of Oxford
Glasgow	Glasgow Museums and Art Galleries
Edinburgh	The Edinburgh University Collection of Historical Wind Instruments
Vienna	Kunsthistorisches Museum, Sammlung alter Musikinstrumente
Brussels	Musée Instrumental du Conservatoire Royal de Musique
The Hague	Gemeente Museum
Paris	Musée Instrumental du Conservatoire National Supérieur de Musique
Stockholm	Musikmuseet
Copenhagen	Musikhistorisk og Carl Claudius' Musikhistoriske Samling
Berlin	Musikinstrumenten-Museum des Staatlichen Instituts für Musikforschung
Munich	Stadtmuseum; Deutsches Museum
Nuremberg	Germanisches Nationalmuseum
Leipzig	Musikinstrumenten Museum, Universität Leipzig
St Petersburg	Institute for Theatre, Music, and Cinematography
Washington, DC	Dayton C. Miller Collection at the Library of Congress Smithsonian Institution
New York	Metropolitan Museum of Art
Boston	Museum of Fine Arts
Vermillion, SD	Shrine to Music Museum at the University of South Dakota
New Haven	Yale University Collection of Musical Instruments

Some of these museums publish plans or measured drawings of some of their instruments. These plans are available for purchase and should provide enough information to enable instrument-makers to fashion replicas of the instruments.

Of special interest to the history of the flute is the Dayton C. Miller Collection in Washington, DC. Miller was a distinguished scientist and acoustician who amassed a collection of over 1,500 flutes, starting in about 1880 and continuing until his death in 1941. It is the largest collection of historical flutes in existence and contains rare and important specimens covering virtually every aspect of the flute.

In addition to these public collections, there are many outstanding private collections of flutes. Fine examples of rare flutes by the great makers are zealously sought after by a number of knowledgeable collectors, many of whom are willing to allow instrument-makers to measure their fine instruments with an eye towards making replicas.

Reprints and Translations of Treatises into English

A development of practical importance soon after the Second World War was the first appearance in English translation of a number of the most influential treatises concerning the performance of eighteenth-century music.

1948   Leopold Mozart's *A Treatise on the Fundamental Principles of Violin Playing* was published for the first time in English translation by Editha Knocker (Oxford University Press).

1949   William J. Mitchell's translation of C. P. E. Bach's *Essay on the True Art of Playing Keyboard Instruments* was published in New York (W. W. Norton) and in 1951 in London (Cassell).

1952   A facsimile edition of the 1751 English edition of Francesco Geminiani's *The Art of Playing on the Violin* was published (Oxford University Press).

1966   Faber and Faber published J. J. Quantz's essays, *On Playing the Flute*, edited and translated into English by Edward R. Reilly (American edition, Macmillan, now Schirmer Books).

1968   Two English translations of the treatise by Jacques Hotteterre le Romain appeared simultaneously: David Lasocki's translation (as *Principles of the Flute, Recorder & Oboe*, London: Barrie & Rockliff/ The Cresset Press) and Paul Marshall Douglas's translation (as *Rudiments of the Flute, Recorder and Oboe*, New York: Dover Publications).

The opportunity was now at hand for interested performers to read a number of important original performance-practice treatises in English or in English translation.

Higher Standards of Editions of Music

Most editions of music published in the first half of the twentieth century were quickly recognized by early-music players as being confusing and misleading. The editorial additions of arbitrary articulations and dynamics (not to mention changed notes and entire movements omitted or substituted) became meaningless to players who performed on original instruments and who paid attention to the styles suggested by the original treatises. The Second World War had forced the cessation of virtually all serious music publishing, so the years following the war were an opportunity to create new editions based upon current standards of musicological scholarship. Among the first of these was the Neue Bach-Ausgabe, the new comprehensive edition of J. S. Bach's works, published by Bärenreiter. The relevant flute volume, containing the Partita in A minor, four sonatas, and the sonata for two flutes and continuo, appeared in 1963, edited by Hans-Peter Schmitz.

Many players of early music now play from copies of original editions or from reproductions of the composer's autograph. The performer then becomes his or her own 'editor', readily making the many decisions that are necessary to prepare a performance.

One technological development that must be acknowledged as a major tool for early-music players is the perfection of photocopying. This invention has eliminated much laborious copying by hand of manuscripts and old editions.

Instrument-Makers Copying Historical Models

Of the many contributing factors to the growth of early music and the revival of the traverso, one of the most important has been the building of musical instruments based upon historical models. Although Arnold Dolmetsch had already begun to make replica musical instruments in the late nineteenth and early twentieth centuries, the idea didn't really take hold until shortly after the end of the Second World War. In 1949, two Harvard-educated men, Frank Hubbard (1920–76) and William Dowd (b. 1922) established a harpsichord-making workshop in Boston. Dowd had been apprenticed to the Detroit builder, John Challis, and Hubbard had worked for a time at the Dolmetsch workshop in England. Whereas almost all instrument-makers were building imaginary instruments, at best loosely based upon historical models, the Hubbard and

Dowd workshop began to model instruments upon the great surviving examples of keyboard instruments by Blanchet, Taskin, and Hemsch. Hubbard wrote down the fruits of his historical studies in a valuable book, *Three Centuries of Harpsichord Making* (1965).

While Hubbard and Dowd were making their historical replicas in Boston, a German-born Bowdoin-educated man began working for the Boston flute-maker, Verne Q. Powell. He was Friedrich von Huene (b. 1929), who learned some of Powell's skills in the four years that he apprenticed under him (1956–60). In 1960 von Huene left the Powell shop to begin his own venture of making Renaissance and baroque flutes and recorders based upon historical models. A Guggenheim Fellowship (1966–7) enabled him to locate, study, and measure some of the greatest flutes and recorders of the sixteenth to eighteenth centuries. Von Huene quickly established his reputation as an outstanding maker, and his instruments were widely acclaimed for workmanship and performance. The stage was now set for serious flute-players to take up the Renaissance or baroque flute, playing upon replica instruments which approached the quality of the finest antique instruments.

Pitches Other Than A=440

Most of von Huene's early instruments were pitched at A=440. This was the prevailing pitch at the time, even for most early-music specialists. However, in the late 1960s the world-wide body of active early-music specialists began to experiment with pitches other than A=440. Arthur Mendel had published studies on the history of pitch in 1948 and 1955[12] and David Boyden's book on the history of violin playing also described the wide variation in pitches in use in previous centuries.[13] Boyden recommended lowering the tuning of a violin by a semitone to A=415 to bring it closer to historically correct pitches for baroque or classical music. By 1967 two influential Dutch early-music specialists, Gustav Leonhardt and Frans Brüggen, were urging that a pitch of A=415 be adopted for baroque performances, and the professional early-music world almost universally heeded their advice. To tune string instruments to a lower pitch was a relatively simple matter of adjusting the strings. For early flutes, the response to this development was for makers to begin producing replica instruments specifically designed to play at pitches lower than A=440.

---

[12] See Arthur Mendel, 'Pitch in the 16th and Early 17th Centuries' (*Musical Quarterly*, 34 (1948)); 'On the Pitches in Use in Bach's Time' (*Musical Quarterly*, 41 (1955)); 'Pitch in Western Music Since 1500: A Re-examination' (*Acta Musicologica*, 50 (1978)).

[13] David D. Boyden, *The History of Violin Playing from Its Origins to 1761 and Its Relationship to the Violin and Violin Music* (London: Oxford University Press, 1965).

2

The Renaissance Flute

(by Anne Smith)

THE increasing interest in early music in general, and in the baroque flute in particular, has in recent years carried over to the Renaissance flute. This instrument is, however, very different from the baroque flute. Perhaps it is just because it appears so deceptively simple that it has long been neglected. In fact it is only recently that a comprehensive study of the extant instruments has been made. This research indicates that the instruments have certain characteristics in common which are quite distinct from those of later flutes. In order to do justice to the instrument, and thus to the music performed on it, the player must be aware of these inherent features, and accept them.

For the purposes of this book, the Renaissance flute will be considered to be the transverse flute in use in Europe between 1500 and the advent of the 'baroque' flute around 1670.

The Instrument

Information concerning the Renaissance flute—an instrument with a more or less cylindrical bore, six finger-holes, and a mouth-hole—is relatively sparse and must be drawn from a number of sources: iconography, inventories, the instruments themselves, descriptions of their use, and musical treatises.[1]

I would like to express my thanks to Barthold Kuijken for his careful perusal of the first version of this chapter and his many valuable questions and suggestions. Kate Clark deserves special mention because of her insistence on clarity, in particular on the subject of Agricola and transposition. In addition, I would also like to thank Anthony Bailes for pointing out the picture of the *Flute Player* (Fig. 1) to me.

[1] The sparsity of information is reflected by the relatively small amount of secondary literature on the instrument: Joscelyn Godwin, 'The Renaissance Flute', *The Consort*, 28 (1972), 70–81; Raymond Meylan, *La Flûte* (Lausanne: Éditions Payot, 1974) which appeared in an English translation by Alfred Clayton, (Portland, Oregon: Amadeus Press, 1988); Bernard Thomas, 'The Renaissance Flute', *Early Music*, 3 (1975), 2–10; David Munrow, *Instruments of the Middle Ages and Renaissance* (London: Oxford University Press, 1976), 53–6; Anne Smith, 'Die Renaissancequerflöte und ihre Musik, ein Beitrag zur Interpretation der Quellen', *Basler Jahrbuch für historische Musikpraxis*, 2 (1978), 9–76; Jane Bowers, '*Flaüste traverseinne* and *Flute d'Allemagne*— The Flute in France from the Late Middle Ages up through 1702', *Recherches sur la musique française classique*, 19 (1979), 7–49; Howard Mayer Brown, 'The Flute', *The New Grove Dictionary of Music and Musicians*, ed. Stanley Sadie (London: Macmillan, 1980), vi. 664–81; Howard Mayer Brown, 'Notes (and Transposing Notes) on the Transverse Flute in the Early Sixteenth Century', *Journal of the American Musical Instrument Society*, 12 (1986), 5–39; and Nicole Journot, *La Flûte traversière renaissance* (thesis, Centre de Musique Ancienne, Geneva, 1985).

FIG. 1. *Flute Player, c.*1600, attributed to Dirck de Quade van Ravesteyn. (Vienna, Kunsthistorisches Museum, Gemäldegalerie. (Inv. No. 3080)

The flute is rarely found in pictures of the fifteenth century, but is depicted with increasing frequency in those of the sixteenth.[2] These pictures suggest that the flute had a twofold usage, as a military instrument and in chamber music. It is difficult to know today how military flutes differed from those for chamber music. In discussions on this subject, it has been hypothesized that the extant instruments with wider bores, and in some cases quite odd tuning (at least using fingerings from the extant sources), were for military use.[3] On the other hand,

---

[2] Bowers, '*Flaüste traverseinne* and *Flute d'Allemagne*'; Brown, 'Notes'.

[3] Derek Lindo, 'The Renaissance Military Flute', *Renaissance Flute Circle Newsletter*, 1 (1988), 3–5, and Filadelfio Puglisi, 'A Survey of Renaissance Flutes', *Galpin Society Journal*, 41 (1988), 73. The flute in the Historisches Museum, Basle, the wooden flute in the Musikinstrumente Museum, Berlin, and the two flutes in the Landeszeughaus, Graz, all have relatively wide bores.

instruments with a narrower bore would have played more easily in the higher register and produced a more piercing sound which perhaps would have been more suited to military usage. That this may actually have been the case is substantiated by Thoinot Arbeau's remark about the fife's bore having 'the thickness of a pistol bullet', giving it a shrill sound.[4] Arbeau writes that the fifers improvised 'to please themselves' and that it sufficed 'for them to keep time with the sound of the drum'.[5] He included two paradigmatic pieces for fife in his treatise. These are the only extant pieces specifically for military flute from the sixteenth century; we cannot judge today how closely they reflect the improvised reality. Later authors, Praetorius and Mersenne, indicate that different fingerings were used for the military flute from those for instruments used for chamber music and that their range was smaller.[6] The use of the flute in chamber music is considerably better documented; the rest of the chapter will be devoted to this instrument.

In pictures, the flute is usually found together with other instruments in mixed ensembles, although there are a few rare cases where only flutes appear together. As a solo instrument it is often found in allegorical scenes or portraits. Iconographical evidence thus suggests that the instrument was usually used in ensembles, either mixed or 'whole'; this is substantiated by contemporary descriptions of festivities in which flutes were employed.[7] The large number of flutes listed in inventories gives an indication of the popularity of the instrument: the Stuttgart court possessed 220 (1589), Henry VIII 74 (1547), Maria of Hungary more than 50 (1555), Philip II of Spain 54 (1598), and the Accademia Filarmonica in Verona 51 (1628).[8]

Not many of these instruments have survived the ravages of time. Filadelfio Puglisi has assembled a list of forty-three instruments found in museums today.[9] Most instruments are found in Italy, the most important collections probably being those in Verona, with other flutes located in Antwerp, Brussels, Berlin,

---

[4] Thoinot Arbeau, *Orchesographie* (Lengres: Jehan des Preyz, 1589), fo. 17ᵛ; facsimile edn., ed. François Lesure (Geneva: Minkoff Reprint, 1972); English trans. Mary Stewart Evans, with new introduction and notes by Julia Sutton (New York: Dover Publications, 1967), 39.

[5] *Orchesographie*, fos. 17ᵛ–18ʳ; translation, 39.

[6] Michael Praetorius, *Syntagma musicum* (Wolfenbüttel; Elias Holwein, 1619), ii; facsimile edn. (Kassel: Bärenreiter, 1958) 22 and 35; and Marin Mersenne, *Harmonie universelle* (Paris: Sebastien Cramoisy, 1636), iii; facsimile edn., ed. François Lesure (Paris: Éditions du Centre National de la Recherche Scientifique, 1965), 243–4.

[7] Brown, 'Notes', 5–10; Smith, 'Die Renaissancequerflöte', 10–12.

[8] Anthony Baines, 'Two Cassel Inventories', *Galpin Society Journal*, 4 (1951), 35; Gustav Bossert, 'Die Hofkapelle unter Eberhard III., 1628–1657', *Württembergische Vierteljahrhefte für Landesgeschichte*, 21 (1912), 133–7; Marcello Castellani, 'Two Late-Renaissance Transverse Flutes', *Galpin Society Journal*, 25 (1972), 74; and Edmond van der Straeten, *La Musique aux Pays-Bas* (Brussels: G. A. van Trigt, 1885), vii. 439–44, viii. 306–7.

[9] Puglisi, 'A Survey of Renaissance Flutes', 67–82.

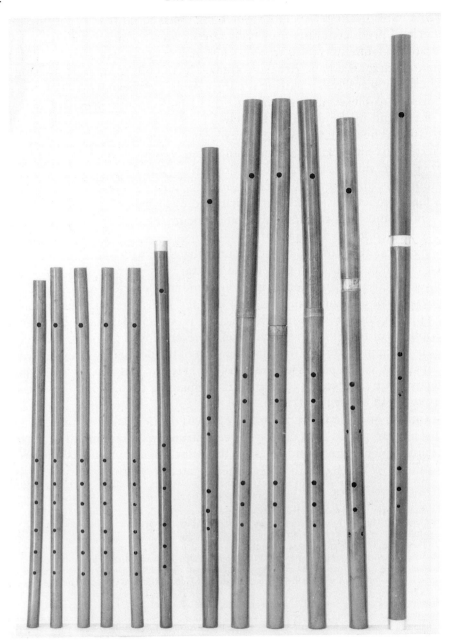

FIG. 2. The Renaissance flutes in the Accademia Filarmonica, Verona. Photo courtesy of Rainer Weber

Vienna, Graz, Bologna, Milan, Meran, Linz, New York, Rome, St Petersburg, and Basle. There seem to be two basic sizes of extant flutes, tenors and basses (although it is difficult to say where one size stops and the other begins). Few instruments still smaller in size exist today.[10] This may be an indication (1) that smaller flutes were used less in Italy, (2) that they gradually fell out of use, or (3) that the survival rate of small instruments is lower than that of larger instruments.

Puglisi examined a large number of these surviving instruments and has come up with certain characteristics shared by the majority of them.[11]

1. The mouth-hole is usually ovoid with the long axis across the flute and rotated slightly clockwise. Its diameter is normally smaller than on baroque instruments.

2. The walls of the instrument, which has a more or less cylindrical bore, taper on the outside from the mouth-hole, the thickest point, towards each end.

3. To facilitate fingering the instrument, the holes were grouped in two sets of three. The spacing between the upper three holes is more or less the same as that between the lower three. The player could choose whether to play with the left hand or the right hand closer to the embouchure hole.[12]

4. On tenors the distance from the upper end of the flute to the mouth-hole is more or less equal to that between the last finger-hole and the lower end of the flute.

5. The ratio of the speaking length of a tenor instrument to the diameter of its bore lies between 30 and 33, that of a bass is somewhat lower.

6. Due to their thin walls, the flutes are very light, tenors weighing from 90 to 170 grams, depending on pitch and type of wood.

There was no international standard pitch level at the time; the pitch varied from place to place, from church to church. This is reflected by the extant instruments. Among the surviving flutes, however, two pitch areas are more frequently represented than others—one larger group of instruments centres around A=410 and a smaller one around A=435.

Certain general pitch levels often seem, none the less, to have been prevalent in a given geographical area. Indeed, often two different pitch levels, one a

---

[10] Puglisi has only found one in Brussels which meets the criteria he has established for Renaissance flutes.

[11] Ibid.

[12] Martin Agricola, *Musica instrumentalis deudsch* (Wittenberg: Georg Rhau, 1545); photo-reprint, ed. Robert Eitner (Leipzig: Breitkopf & Härtel, 1896), fo. 25ʳ, shows a picture of a flute indicating that the right hand was responsible for the three holes closer to the embouchure hole, the left hand for those further away. In his first edition, *Musica instrumentalis deudsch*, (Wittenberg: George Rhau, 1529); facsimile edn. (Hildesheim: George Olms Verlag, 1969), fo. vʳ, however, he said that the player was free to choose which hand went where.

whole tone higher than the other, seem to have coexisted within a specific region. Praetorius writes, for example, that in Prague and several other Catholic areas there were two pitch levels: *Kammerton* for 'the table and other convivial occasions', and *Chorton*, a whole tone lower, for church music.[13] This whole tone difference in pitch may also be observed in entries in some inventories of that time, as well as in modern collections of instruments.[14] Flutes and mute-cornetts often seem to have played at the lower of these two pitches (as reflected by the group of flutes around A=410) and there are indications that strings (plucked and bowed) preferred this lower pitch.[15]

In buying instruments today, it is important to obtain real copies, ones that are based on actual measurements, having the features mentioned above, rather than fantasy instruments. The originals, for the most part, are truly gratifying to play. We need to learn far more from them before venturing to improve on them.

Two deviations from the originals are particularly common and should be avoided in purchasing an instrument. First of all, many makers have tried to make transverse tenor recorders, i.e. instruments with the characteristics of a tenor recorder but with the embouchure of a transverse flute; like tenor recorders these instruments have a range of about one and a half octaves from the lowest note. The d' transverse flute, however, as we shall discuss later, could take the function of the tenor, alto, and even descant voice in a 'whole' consort. A range of one and a half octaves would clearly not accommodate the demands of all these roles. Thus in buying an instrument one should pay attention to its entire range and in particular to the two octaves used most frequently, namely from g' to g'''. Secondly, some makers have tried to make Renaissance flutes with 'modern' fingerings, something which goes against the essence of the instrument and only creates new problems.

The Sources

The following treatises, listed in chronological order, give us what specific information we have about playing the Renaissance flute, about the sizes used (i.e. descant, alto/tenor, bass), its range, and its fingerings.[16]

[13] Praetorius, *Syntagma musicum*, ii. 15.

[14] For example, see Bossert, 'Die Hofkapelle unter Eberhard III. 1628–1657', 134–5, and Rainer Weber, 'Some Researches into Pitch in the 16th Century with Particular Reference to the Instruments in the Accademia Filarmonica of Verona', *Galpin Society Journal*, 28 (1975), 7–10.

[15] Weber, 'Some Researches'; Smith, 'Die Renaissancequerflöte', 25–8; and Anne Smith, 'Belege zur Frage der Stimmtonhöhe bei Michael Praetorius', *Alte Musik: Praxis und Reflexion* (Winterthur: Amadeus Verlag, 1983).

[16] For a more complete discussion of the sources see Smith, 'Die Renaissancequerflöte'. The translations here are by the author.

- Sebastian Virdung, *Musica getutscht* (Basle: Michael Furter, 1511), fos. Biii^v and [Civ]^v; facsimile edn., ed. Klaus Wolfgang Niemöller (Kassel: Bärenreiter, 1970).
  He is the first theorist to mention the flute in the sixteenth century. He has a picture of a single 'Zwerchpfeiff'; later it becomes clear that for him it is a military instrument.

- Martin Agricola, *Musica instrumentalis deudsch* (Wittenberg: Georg Rhau, 1529), fos. xii^r–xivv^r; facsimile edn., (Hildesheim: Georg Olms Verlag, 1969).[17]
  Agricola is the first to discuss a consort of 'Schweizerpfeiffen'. Here he gives fingering charts for a bass in D, tenor/alto in A, and descant in e (see Appendix to this chapter). The range of each instrument is said to be three octaves, greater than that mentioned by any other author.

  He also writes that one should play with vibrato: 'If you want to have a fundament, learn to pipe with trembling breath, for it greatly embellishes the melody' (fo. xii^r). He is alone in mentioning the use of a diaghragmatic vibrato, as opposed to finger vibrato, in the sixteenth century. It is not referred to again in flute tutors until the second half of the eighteenth century.

- Martin Agricola, *Musica instrumentalis deudsch* (Wittenberg, Georg Rhau, 1545), fos. 24^r–31^v; photo-reprint, ed. Robert Eitner, *Publikation älterer praktischer und theoretischer Musikwerke xxiv/20* (Leipzig: Breitkopf & Härtel, 1896).
  This edition contains two sets of fingering charts for flutes, one set in C, G, and d, and the other in GG, D, and A. The flutes are given ranges between two octaves plus a second and two octaves plus a sixth (see Appendix). The first set is in the main section on the flute. Above the chart for the descant flute, however, appears the following caption: 'Three irregular scales of these flutes follow, [which have been] transposed up a fourth.' In introducing the second set of charts ('three other regular scales for these flutes'), which—for some inexplicable reason—is separated from the main section on the flute by a discussion of the large pipes ('gros pfeiffen'), i.e. trumpets and trombones (fos. 28^v–29^r), Agricola explains the necessity for the various charts:

Don't let yourself be irritated that I now speak of two [fundaments, i.e. fingering charts] and spoke of a third one previously in the Deudschen Instrumental (1529). For here one can transpose the Scalas [the scales of the instrument] as in singing, note that, just as one does it on organs or lutes, as I have told you before, and on the others [instruments] . . . Take the one which you prefer; but I wish to say that in general, this one seems to me to be the most comfortable [GG, D, A]. (fo. 29^v)

---

[17] There is an English translation of the section on recorders and flutes in this and the following work by Agricola in William E. Hettrick, 'Martin Agricola's Poetic Discussion of the Recorder and Other Woodwind Instruments', *The American Recorder*, 21 (1980), 103–13; 23 (1982), 139–46; and 24 (1983), 51–60.

Again Agricola suggests using vibrato on the flute, this time with a reference to the vibrato used in Polish violin-playing (fo. 26ʳ).

- Philibert Jambe de Fer, *L'Epitome musical* (Lyons: Michel du Bois, 1556), 47–55; facsimile edn., ed. François Lesure, *Annales musicologiques*, 6 (1958–63), 341–86.

Jambe de Fer gives the range of the bass flute as G–g′, that of the tenor as d–g″ or a″, the upper three or four notes being forced. In the section on recorders he writes that, in contrast to the traverse flutes, the upper part is not played by the same size instrument as is used for the tenor and alto. This implies that for Jambe de Fer the flute consort consisted of one G bass and three instruments in d (notated pitch). He mentions that flat modes are more pleasant, easy, and natural than sharp ones. He also makes the following remarks on how to play the instrument:

> One must learn the art and manner of placing the flute exactly in the middle of the lower lip [blowing] with a soft and moderate wind, increasing it little by little in order to ascend; for descending one must lessen it little by little following the line of the music without being afraid of advancing the lips. Also I want to warn you that playing [the flute] is impossible for those who have no tongue, just as speaking is, for all notes that are spoken must be led by the tongue; therefore, those of you who take pleasure in playing [the flute] should guard your tongue against mould, which is to say, drink often. (p. 51)

- Lodovico Zacconi, *Prattica di musica* (Venice, 1592), fo. 218ʳ⁻ᵛ; facsimile edn. (Bologna: Forni Editore, [1967]).

Zacconi, in a discussion of the ranges of most of the instruments of his time, gives that of the flute as d–d″.

- Aurelio Virgiliano, *Il Dolcimelo*, Bk. 3 (after 1600), p. [109]; facsimile edn., ed. Marcello Castellani (Florence: Studio per Edizioni Scelte, 1979).

This treatise contains a fingering chart for a flute with a range from d to a″ (see Appendix, p. 30). It also indicates the possibility of transposing a fourth higher or a fourth or fifth lower.

- Michael Praetorius, *Syntagma musicum* (Wolfenbüttel: Elias Holwein, 1619), ii. 22 and 35, iii. 156–7; facsimile edn., (Kassel: Bärenreiter, 1958).[18]

In the main text Praetorius gives the flute a range of nineteen notes, fifteen natural ones and four flageolet tones (ii. 35). Only one flute is given this range

---

[18] There is an English translation of the section on instruments by Harold Blumenfeld (New York, 1962) as well as of the entire second volume, *Syntagma Musicum II: Organographia Parts I and II*, trans. and ed. David Z. Crookes (Oxford: Clarendon Press, 1986); Oxford Early Music Series 7.

in his diagram, that in d′; this suggests that this size flute was the one primarily used in his time. The instrument in a′ is only given a range of two octaves; its highest note, a‴, is the same as the highest one given for the flute in d′. For the first time the ranges of the instruments are given at sounding pitch; Praetorius writes that the flute, like the recorder, was played an octave higher than notated, although many people appeared not to notice this distinction (ii. 21; see below for further discussion of this point). In discussing instrumentation, he mentions that flat modes are better for the flute than sharp ones. From what he says further, it seems clear that the pieces specified by him as being appropriate for three flutes and a bass instrument should be played on three flutes in d′ (iii. 156–7, cf. Jambe de Fer).

- Marin Mersenne, *Harmonie universelle* (Paris: Sebastien Cramoisy, 1636), iii. 241–4; facsimile edn., ed. François Lesure (Paris: Édition du Centre National de la Recherche Scientifique, 1965).[19]
Mersenne gives two fingering charts, one for a g and one for a d′ flute (see Appendix); Mersenne, too, notates the ranges of the flute at sounding pitch. These charts differ significantly from one another. Unfortunately, Mersenne himself says that it is difficult to give the true reason for this difference.
   He writes that one does not usually play all parts of a piece on flute, because of the bass being difficult to play due to its size. A trombone, serpent, or some other bass instrument was used for the bass.

- Pierre Trichet, *Le traité des instruments de musique* (after 1638), ed. François Lesure, *Annales musicologiques*, 3 (1955), 332–49.
Trichet, in the chapter about the flute, concerns himself mainly with the use of the flute by the ancient Greeks and Romans. He does, however, make a few comments about the contemporary transverse flute.

- Jacob van Eyck, *Der Fluyten Lust-hof* (Amsterdam: Paulus Matthysz, 1646), foreword; facsimile edn., ed. Kees Otten (Amsterdam: B. V. Muziekhandel Saul B. Groen, n.d.).
According to the preface, the music in this collection may be played not only on the c′ recorder (notated pitch)—as one so often hears it done today—but also on a flute in g. Van Eyck gives the range of the flute as g–d‴. He follows the older practice of notating the ranges of the instruments an octave lower than sounding pitch. The whole range of the flute is thus a fourth higher than that most often cited in the other sources. The choice of such small instruments indicates that van Eyck desired an unusually high tessitura for his pieces.

---

[19] There is an English translation of the book on instruments by R. E. Chapman (The Hague, 1957).

Conclusions Drawn from These Sources

First of all, the instrument was generally given a range of two octaves plus a fourth or fifth. Jambe de Fer, to be sure, writes that the bass flute is limited to two octaves. In any case, it is a much larger range than has often been assumed, and is required in some of the pieces explicitly designated for flute, such as the ricercate by Aurelio Virgiliano and certain pieces from the English consort repertoire.[20]

Characteristic for most of these sources is that the range of the flute, just like the recorder at that time, is notated an octave lower than it actually sounds. Praetorius was the first to point out this discrepancy. He writes the following about the pitch of the recorders and flutes:

It is commonly thought by numerous musicians that this kind of recorder or flute [in c or d respectively] is a true tenor in pitch, and that their lowest note is the note c or d in the tenor [𝄢 ♩ ○] and that thus their pitch is at four foot (according to the mensuration of the organ makers). To tell the truth I was of the same opinion at the beginning, because it is very difficult for the ear to recognize and distinguish the difference; but when one plays this note against that of an organ pipe and assiduously compares one with the other, [one hears that] it is only a true descant, as the note c′ or d′ [𝄞 ♩ ○] is at two foot pitch. (ii. 21)

Praetorius is thus the first explicitly to give the ranges of the instruments of the flute family at sounding pitch.

In his discussion of the instrumentation of motets of his time, Praetorius also gives examples of music in g-treble, soprano, mezzo-soprano, and alto clefs which he considers most suitable for flutes in d′ (iii. 156–7). As ledger lines were avoided in Renaissance vocal music, the customary range of parts notated in these clefs would be d′–g″ for g-treble clef; b(♭)–e(♭)″ for soprano clef; g–c″ for mezzo-soprano clef; and e(♭)–a′ for alto clef (see Example 1). Thus one was expected to play from a notated e(♭?) to a notated g″ on a flute whose lowest note was a sounding d′. This makes the necessity of playing an octave higher than notated pitch completely obvious, because if one were to play a d′ notated just below the lowest line in a g-treble clef by using the fingering for the lowest note on a d′ flute, one would no longer be able to play the parts notated in the

Ex. 1

---

[20] The range of Virgiliano's Ricercata 12, for example, is f–f″; that of the flute part of 'The Lady Frances Sidneys Goodnight' by Richard Allison (in the *Walsingham Consort Books*) is d–c″.

still lower clefs. The fact that the entire compass of the d′ flute, as Praetorius suggests, really was used in the sixteenth century, is corroborated by the few above-mentioned pieces for flute with a very large range.

The discrepancy between the notation and the actual sounding pitch is also evident if one closely examines the information found in the fingering charts and applies it to the ranges of the pieces specifically designated for flute. As a consequence, in choosing music for Renaissance flutes, one must always take into account the necessity of playing an octave higher than the notated pitch.

Comparing the fingering charts found in the sources (see Appendix), one discovers they are for the most part in agreement. Only Mersenne's second chart differs consistently from the others and he himself writes that he does not know why it is so different. Otherwise there are only a few notes which exhibit significant variants: c″, f♯″, b″, c‴, d‴, e‴, g‴, a‴ (sounding pitch, i.e. one octave higher than notated). These notes all have something in common: they are all difficult to play in tune and their tuning varies more from instrument to instrument than others. For these notes, then, one has to find the fingerings which work best on each individual flute. On the other hand, there is considerable agreement that the fingering for a″ (sounding pitch) requires the three fingers of the right hand. Without these fingers it is much too low, with them it is too high. Apparently the sound of the higher version was preferred and the player was expected to correct the intonation. In general, it is necessary to correct intonation to a far greater degree than one is accustomed to do in playing later instruments. When working on intonation one has to keep in mind that a mean-tone temperament was generally accepted at the time, a tuning in which the major thirds are purer than in later temperaments. Lastly, there is the problem of e♭″, which requires a half-hole and is usually weak. It is simply something one has to come to terms with and, more importantly, practise.

In the sixteenth century there were two documented ways in which flutes were utilized in 'whole consort', that is to say with all parts being played on flutes. For Agricola the consort consisted of three different sizes of instruments. In the second edition of *Musica instrumentalis deudsch* of 1545 he provides fingering charts for each of the three flutes, depicting their respective 'regular' lowest pitches or fundamentals as GG for the longest or bass flute, D for the middle-sized flute which could fulfil both the function of the alto and the tenor, and A for the smallest or descant flute (fos. 29ᵛ–31ᵛ; see Example 2, in which the fundamentals of the sizes of flute mentioned in this chapter are shown in

Ex. 2

GG C D G A c d e g c′ d′ a′

staff notation). Another set of fingering charts (1545, fos. 26ᵛ–28ʳ) depicts the three flutes as having a different set of fundamentals, namely C, G and d, that is, a fourth higher than the regular ones; yet another (1529, fos. 8ᵛ–9ʳ) shows them as having fundamentals of D, A, and e, a fifth higher than the regular ones. It is clear that Agricola did not mean to say that one used seven different sizes of flute when playing in consort; there were only three. He depicted them as having three different sets of fundamentals—a 'regular' set and two others—merely to aid the performer in transposing; to transpose up a fourth or a fifth on the tenor/alto flute, for example, the player could simply envisage the instrument as having a fundamental of A or G respectively, instead of D.

As Howard Mayer Brown has pointed out, these three sets of fingering charts correspond to the following automatic transpositions: music played on flutes envisioned to have GG, D, and A as their fundamentals would be transposed up two octaves in relation to its notation; imagining the flutes to be in C, G, and d would result in a transposition of an octave and a fifth higher; and, finally, imagining them to be in D, A, and e would result in a transposition of an octave and a fourth higher.[21]

It must be mentioned, however, that the set of fundamentals understood by Agricola to represent the 'regular' (and 'most comfortable') way of using the instruments is an octave lower than those mentioned by other theorists, and thus two octaves lower than notated pitch. One suspects that this is due to some confusion on the part of Agricola related to the problems of transposition and the normal octave difference between notated and sounding pitch on the Renaissance flute. The fact that he gives one transposition in the first edition and two different ones in the second edition, in which the regular combination for some odd reason comes after the irregular one, suggests that he had little personal knowledge of how the instruments were employed, but instead had gathered bits and pieces of information from various players which he then tried to piece together in some sort of orderly way. This presumably led him to notate erroneously the regular combination of flutes an octave lower than was otherwise the practice; even today the subject of the Renaissance flute and transposition always seems to involve mental acrobatics.

Two considerations should be kept in mind when choosing which transposition is best for a specific piece of music. First of all, one should make sure that each part of the composition lies in the best possible range of the flute which is to play it. Secondly, one should try to see that none of the instruments is constantly forced to play notes that are awkward on the instrument. Specifically this means that one wants to avoid having the fingering which is a minor second

---

[21] Brown, 'Notes', 22–9.

or ninth above the lowest note of the flute (i.e. eb′ or eb″ on a d′ flute) be a part of the diatonic scale of the piece concerned, as this fingering produces a very weak sound. This fingering, which involves closing the bottom hole half-way, is good enough for occasional passing and neighbour tones, but one would not want to have such notes appear prominently throughout a piece. In addition, experience has shown that on the higher flutes in the ensemble one wants to avoid having the fingering which is a major third or tenth above the lowest note of the instrument (i.e. f♯′ or f♯″ on an instrument in d′) be the third of the mode of the piece one is playing. Having this fingering appear frequently as the third of the mode tends to create serious intonation problems within the ensemble. Thus the transposition chosen for a specific piece of music would need to take not only the range of the parts into consideration, but also the mode of the composition. Therefore if one observes these limitations in putting the transpositions suggested by Agricola into practice, pieces in G and C modes with major thirds and in E, A, and D modes with minor thirds may be played with the GG-D-D-A (or possibly G-d-d-a) combination and would sound two octaves (or one) higher than notated pitch; pieces in F and C modes with major thirds and in G, D, and A modes with a minor third may be played with the C-G-G-d combination and would sound an octave and a fifth higher than notated; and pieces in G modes with a major third and in A and E modes with a minor third may be played with the D-A-A-e combination, and would sound an octave and a fourth higher than notated pitch.

When reconstructing a consort of this nature with instruments of three different sizes, one is faced with the problem that the highest flute must of necessity be built to scale due to the dearth of high original flutes.

The second documented way of utilizing flutes in playing in 'whole' consort was first described by Jambe de Fer in 1556. He wrote that a d′ flute was also used to play the top part. He clearly states that a flute ensemble consisted of a g bass and three d′ flutes for the tenor, alto, and descant (sounding pitch). This means that the pieces performed by a flute consort must of necessity lie rather high. Mersenne writes that the bass was often played by some other instrument, because of the awkwardness of the low flute.

All the later sources assume that the top part was normally played on a d′ flute. The only exception is van Eyck, and he obviously wanted a still higher sound colour (as is also clear from his choice of the soprano recorder). It may therefore be assumed that whenever a flute is referred to in the last half of the sixteenth and beginning of the seventeenth century, an instrument in d′ is intended unless otherwise explicitly stated. This is thus the appropriate size flute for solo diminutions and similar virtuoso pieces of the time.

Jambe de Fer and Praetorius mention that the flat modes are more appropriate for flute. This is born out by most of the pieces where flute is specifically called for, with the exception of the English consort repertory. Experience has also shown that in a consort using three d′ flutes intonation and sound quality is usually better in flat modes, in spite of the difficulties with e♭″.

The Music

In the Renaissance the instrumentation of a piece of music was rarely fixed. Decisions concerning how a piece was to be performed were made on the basis of convention, of the availability of instruments and musicians, and of taste. To discover how the flute was generally employed at that time, it is necessary to study the music which calls for it and co-ordinate the information derived from it with that found in the theoretical sources. A list of works for flute is found in the author's article on the flute.[22] It includes two Attaingnant prints of French chansons, some German songs published by Georg Forster, various and sundry pieces for mixed ensembles by German and Italian composers, solo ricercate by Virgiliano, and the works for English consort. These works show the divers ways in which the flute was utilized.

To begin with, they were used in 'whole consort'. As discussed above, there are two documented ways of doing this, one using three sizes as mentioned by Agricola, and the other later method of grouping of a bass in g with three tenors in d′ (sounding pitch).

Attaingnant published two prints in 1533 in which he has marked some pieces as being particularly suitable for flutes, some being particularly suitable for recorders, and the rest as working well on both instruments. The ranges of the parts in the pieces for flutes extend somewhat higher for the most part than those in the works for recorders; most of the pieces for flutes are in flat keys. Howard Mayer Brown recommends that, as Agricola is the only contemporary theorist writing about playing flutes in consort, one should consider using three different sizes of instruments and Agricola's suggestions for transposition in performing these works.[23] Two things speak against using this older grouping, however. First of all, Agricola was writing in Germany and it is by no means certain that the instruments were employed in the same way there as in France. For example, Howard Mayer Brown quotes François Scépeaux, sieur de Vielleville and maréchal of France, as saying in 1554 that 'he could not understand why the instrument was called a German flute, "for the French play them better and more musically than any other nation; and they are never

[22] Smith, 'Die Renaissancequerflöte', 52–60.   [23] Brown, 'Notes', 31–9.

played *a 4* in Germany, as they normally are in France"'.[24] Jambe de Fer, although he was certainly writing about how the instruments were used in France, only published his treatise twenty-three years after the appearance of the Attaingnant prints. Thus the manner in which flutes were employed in France may have changed between the date of the appearance of the Attaingnant prints and the time he was writing. On the other hand, it is well known that theory often reflects a slightly earlier practice; therefore the use of the more modern consort described by Jambe de Fer may already have been in vogue in France at the time of the Attaingnant prints. Secondly, the works suited for recorder require no transposition. There seems to be no reason why the works for one kind of instrument in the print should need transposition when the works for the others do not. The ranges and the modes of the pieces, however, do correspond with that which is described by later theorists (such as Jambe de Fer and Michael Praetorius) as being particularly suitable for flutes; this suggests that the pieces for flutes in the Attaingnant prints may justifiably be played on the more modern combination of one g and three d' instruments.

In choosing other works for a flute consort, one first has to decide whether one is going to play them with three sizes of flute or two. If one is using a consort of three sizes of instruments, one should then—taking the mode of the composition and range of the parts into consideration—apply the appropriate transposition suggested by Agricola. For the more modern grouping of one g bass with three d' tenors, it is preferable to stay in the flat keys as there will be fewer intonation problems. With this more modern grouping of instruments, it is particularly important to check the range of each part carefully. The lower parts must be fairly high; the top voice, however, is limited usually only by the performer's capabilities.

The flute also often played an inner part (up an octave) in a larger mixed consort. Here the top part was often played by a violin or mute-cornett. Praetorius, in particular, made many suggestions of how the flute could be used in this manner in large, often multi-chorus, sacred works.[25] One special form of this mixed consort was found in England, where the flute was joined by a violin, lute, cittern, pandora, and bass gamba. Here, too, it played an inner part up an octave, most often the alto. Although it goes against the grain of the modern musician to have a secondary part be heard above the melody, it is something that should not just be rejected out of hand. Experience shows that it brings out other aspects of the compositions; it does, however, place quite different demands on the flautist.

---

[24] Brown, 'Notes, 12.
[25] Cf. Michael Praetorius, *Gesamtausgabe der musikalischen Werke*, 17 (Wolfenbüttel).

Ricercata
per Trauer-
ta, Violino,
Cornetto, et
altri Instru-
menti.

FIG. 3. Ricercata 6 from Virgiliano's *Il Dolcimelo*, Libro secondo, after 1600; the MS
is in Bologna, Civico Museo bibliografico musicale (Ms. C. 33)

Recommended Editions

Modern editions of the pieces specifically for flute are listed in the author's article, 'Die Renaissancequerflöte' (see n. 1).

Pierre Attaingnant, *Fourteen Chansons* (1533), London Pro Musica (PC1). It contains the works in the second Attaingnant print for recorders, as well as those for flutes or recorders.

Giovanni Bassano, *Ricercate/Passaggi et Cadentie*, ed. Richard Erig, Musikverlang zum Pelikan (Italian Diminution Tutors 1).

Aurelio Virgiliano, *Thirteen Ricercate from Il Dolcimelo*, London Pro Musica (REP1).

Italienische Diminutionen, ed. Richard Erig and Veronika Gutmann, (Zurich, 1979) (Prattica Musicale 1).

Thomas Morley, *The First Book of Consort Lessons* (London, 1599 and 1611); modern ed., ed. Sidney Beck (New York: Peters, 1959).

Music for Mixed Consort, ed. Warwick Edwards (London, 1977) (Musica Britannica 40).

London Pro Musica publishes many practical and inexpensive collections of Renaissance music. Particularly noteworthy is the series Ricercate e Passaggi (REP), which publishes diminutions in a practical form.

Corpus Mensurabilis Musicae, ed. Armen Carapetyan, published by the American Institute of Musicology, is an important source of Renaissance music. The complete works of numerous composers appear in this series.

Style

As there is little written about style in the flute sources, one is forced to turn to more general vocal and instrumental treatises. From them one learns that the voice was the ideal 'instrument', and that therefore a 'singing' style should be cultivated. Unfortunately there are no extant Renaissance singers, so our information on style must be culled from the theoretical sources and from the music itself. Two aspects of style are of primary importance to the flautist, articulation and the art of diminution.

In the Renaissance musicians attempted to make the instruments speak just as clearly as the voice in speech or song (cf. Jambe de Fer). Each note, including even the fastest note values in the most complex embellishments, received a syllable of its own. As in ordinary speech, however, the articulation varied in clarity and strength, with longer note values receiving greater stress and the fast ones less. Various syllables were used to achieve this differentiation, *te*, *de*, *re*, *le*, and *ke* being the most common. Each form of musical motion had a combination of syllables best suited to it. The *lingua riversa* was of particular importance, an especially soft tonguing for the fastest passages. It is discussed in detail, along with other kinds of articulation found in the sixteenth- and early seventeenth-century sources dealing with wind instruments, in the introduction to *Italienische Diminutionen* (which has an English translation) listed in the bibliography below.

During the course of the sixteenth century, instrumentalists, copying a practice of the singers, began to improvise embellishments to their parts. These dimimutions became in time quite ornate, requiring great virtuosity on the part of the musicians. Various authors wrote tutors on the art of diminution which include examples of how to proceed from one interval to the next as well as embellishments of the upper voice of entire pieces. These diminutions are not for any specific instrument but are intended to serve as models for learning how to improvise in this style. They thus have much to offer the present-day Renaissance flautist. The solo ricercate by Virgiliano or Bassano can also be seen in this light, as exercises designed to introduce the flourishes needed in improvisation.[26] Improvised ornamentation was thus an integral part of Renais-

---

[26] Imogene Horsley, 'The Solo Ricercar in Diminution Manuals: New Light on Early Wind and String Techniques', *Acta Musicologica*, 33 (1961), 29–40.

sance performance practice and as such should be cultivated when playing music and instruments of the period.

Bibliography of Renaissance Performance Practice

The following works are suggested as an introduction to the subject. In them further bibliographic information will be found.

Howard Mayer Brown, 'Performing Practice', *The New Grove Dictionary of Music and Musicians*, ed. Stanley Sadie (London: Macmillan, 1980), xiv. 370–93.

Howard Mayer Brown, *Embellishing Sixteenth-Century Music* (Early Music Series, 1; London: Oxford University Press, 1976). It not only contains information about florid improvisation, but also about other aspects of Renaissance performance practice.

Italienische Diminutionen, ed. Richard Erig and Veronika Gutmann (Prattica Musicale, 1; Zurich: Amadeus Verlag, 1979).

Imogene Horsley, 'Improvised Embellishment in the Performance of Renaissance Polyphonic Music', *Journal of the American Musicological Society*, 4 (1951), 3–19.

Imogene Horsley, 'Wind Techniques in the Sixteenth and Early Seventeenth Centuries', *Brass Quarterly*, 4 (1960), 49–63.

Elizabeth V. Phillips and John-Paul Christopher Jackson, *Performing Medieval and Renaissance Music: An Introductory Guide* (New York: Schirmer Books, 1986).

APPENDIX

Comparative Fingering Charts

The fingerings for all sizes of flute have been adapted to the d flute to facilitate comparison. The sounding pitches have been indicated to avoid confusion.

			d′	e♭′	e′
1a	Agricola 1529	D	●●●●●●		●●●●●○
b	Agricola 1529	A	●●●●●●	●●●●●♭	●●●●●○
c	Agricola 1529	e	●●●●●●	●●●●●♭	●●●●●○
2a	Agricola 1545	C	●●●●●●		●●●●●○
b	Agricola 1545	G	●●●●●●		●●●●●○
c	Agricola 1545	d	●●●●●●		●●●●●○
3a	Agricola 1545	GG	●●●●●●		●●●●●○
b	Agricola 1545	D	●●●●●●		●●●●●○
c	Agricola 1545	A	●●●●●●		●●●●●○
4	Jambe de Fer 1556	G[1]	●●●●●●		●●●●●○
5	Virgiliano after 1600	d	●●●●●●		●●●●●○
6a	Mersenne 1636	g	●●●●●●		●●●●●○
b	Mersenne 1636	d′	●●●●●●		●●●●●○

[1] In his fingering chart Jambe de Fer gives the following advice: 'Le plus bas ton, vent bien doux' ('for the lowest note, very soft breath').

	f′	f♯′	g′	g♯′	a′	b♭′
1a	●●●●○●		●●●○○●		●●○○○●	●○●○●●
b	●●●●○●		●●●○○●	●●◐○○● / ●●○●○○	●●○○○●	●○●○○●
c	●●●●○●	●●●●○○	●●●○○●	●●◐○○● / ●●○●○○	●●○○○●	●○●○○●
2a		●●●●○○	●●●○○○		●●○○○●	
b	●●●●○●	●●●●○○	●●●○○○		●●○○○●	●○●○○●
c	●●●●○●		●●●○○○		●●○○○●	●○●○○●
3a	●●●●○●		●●●○○●		●●○○○●	●○●○○●
b	●●●●○●		●●●○○●		●●○○○●	●○●○○●
c	●●●●○●		●●●○○●		●●○○○●	●○●○○●
4	●●●●○●	●●●●○○	●●●○○○	●●○○●●	●●○○○●	●○●○○●
5	●●●●○●		●●●○○○		●●○○○○	●○●○○○
6a		●●●●○○	●●●○○○		●●○○○○	
b		●●●●○○²	●●●○○●		●●○○○●	

	b	c″	c♯″	d″	e♭″	e″
1a	●○○○○●	○○●●●●		○●●●●●	●●●●●◐	●●●●●○
b		○○●●●●		○●●●●●	●●●●●◐	●●●●●○
c	●○○○○●	○○●●●●		○●●●●●	●●●●●◐	●●●●●○
2a	●○○○○●	○●○○○●	○○○○○●	○●●●●●		●●●●●○
b	●○○○○●	○●○○○●		○●●●●●		●●●●●○
c	●○○○○●	○●○○○●		○●●●●●		●●●●●○
3a	●○○○○●	○○●●●●		○●●●●●		●●●●●○
b	●○○○○●	○○●●●●		○●●●●●	●●●●●◐	●●●●●○
c		○○●●●●		○●●●●●	●●●●●◐	●●●●●○
4	●○○○○●	○●○●○○●³	○○○○○●	○●●●●●		●●●●●○
5		○●○○○○		●●●●●●		●●●●●○
6a	●○○○○○		○○○○○ ○⁴	○●●●●●		●●●●●○
b	●○○○○●	○●●○●●		○○●●●●		○●●●●○

² Mersenne gives this fingering for f′, but it is clear that f♯′ is meant.

³ Jambe de Fer writes 'Aucuns laissent cestuy' ('Some leave this one on') in reference to the ring finger of the right hand.

⁴ Mersenne gives this fingering for f′ (c′), but it is clear that f♯′ (c♯′) is meant.

	f″	f♯″	g″	g♯″	a″	b♭″
1a	●●●●●○●		●●●●○○●	●●○○○○	●●○●●●	●○●●●●
b	●●●●●○●		●●●●○○●	●●φ○○●	●●○●●●	●○●●●●
c	●●●●●○●	●●●●●○●[5]	●●●●○○●	●●○●○○ / ●●φ○○●	●●○●●●	●○●●●●
2a	●●●●●○●	●●●●●○○	●●●○○○		●●○●●●	
b	●●●●●○●	●●●●●○○	●●●○○○		●●○●●●	●○●●●●
c	●●●●●○●		●●●○○○		●●○●●●	●○●●●●
3a	●●●●●○●	●●●●●○○	●●●○○○		●●○●●●	●○●●●●
b	●●●●●○●		●●●○○○		●●○●●●	●○●●●●
c	●●●●●○●		●●●○○○		●●○●●●	●○●●●●
4	●●●●●○●	●●●○●●φ	●●●○○●		●●○●●●●[7]	●○●●●●●[8]
5	●●●●●○●		●●●○○○		●●○●●●	●○●●●●
6a		●●●●○○	●●●○○○		●●○○○○	
b		○●●●○○[6]	○●●○○○		○●●●●●	

	b″	c‴	d‴	e♭‴	e‴	f‴
1a	●○○●●●	○○●●●●	○●●●●●	●●○●○●	●●○○○●	●○○○○●
b		○○●●●●	○●●●●●	●●○●○●	●●○○○● / ●●●○○●	●○○○○●
c	●○○●●●	○○●●●●	○●●●●●	●●○●○●		●○○○○●
2a	●○○●●●	○○○○○●	○●●●●●		●●○○○●	
b	●○○●●●	○○○○○●	○●●●●●		●●○○○●	
c	●○○●●●	○○○○○●	○●●●●●		●●○○○●	●○○○○●
3a	●○○●●●	○○●●●●	○●●●●●		●●○○○●	●○○○○●
b	●○○●●●	○○●●●●	○●●●●●	●●○●○●	●●○○○●	●○○○○●
c		○○●●●●	○●●●●●	●●○●○●	●●○○○●	●○○○○●
4	○●○●●●●[9]	○○○●●●	○●●○●●			
5		○○○●●●	○●●●●●		●●○○●○	●○○○●○
6a	●○○○○○	○○○○●●[10]	○●●●●●		●●○○●●	
b	○○○●●○	○○○●●○	○○●○●●		○●○○●○	○○○○●○[11]

[5] Agricola gives the same fingering for g″ and g♯″ (here f″ and f♯″). The g♯″ should probably be fingered similarly to g♯′.

[6] Mersenne gives this fingering for f″, but it is clear that f♯″ is meant.

[7] Jambe de Fer gives the following advice for this note: 'Vent doux & bien couvert' ('Soft breath and well covered').

[8] This fingering is interchanged in Jambe de Fer's chart with the one indicated for b″.

[9] This fingering is interchanged in Jambe de Fer's chart with the one indicated for b♭″.

[10] Perhaps a fingering for f♯″ (c♯‴)?

[11] Perhaps a fingering for f♯‴?

	f♯'''	g'''	a'''	b'''	c''''	d''''
1a		○○●●●●	○●●●●●	●●○○●●	○○●○●●	○●●●●●
b		○○●●●●	○●●●●●	●●○○●●	○○●○●●	○●●●●●
c		○○●●●●	○●●●●●	●●○○●●	○○●○●●	●●●●●●
2a						
b						
c		○○●●●●				
3a		○○●●●●	○●●●●●			
b		○○●●●●				
c		○○●●●●	○●●●●●	●●○○●●		
4						
5		●○●○●○	○●●●●●			
6a	●●●●○○	●●●○○○	●●○●●●			
b		○●●○○○				

3

The Baroque Flute

THE baroque flute emerged around 1670 and gradually evolved through several stages before becoming the classical flute in the second half of the eighteenth century. While it is easy to describe this evolution in general terms, it is more difficult to be very explicit about its development. Almost no surviving baroque flutes are dated. No baroque flute-maker's diary is known to exist. No patents were issued. We must depend almost entirely upon known working dates of makers, iconography, and a few written commentaries to trace this development.[1]

While the Renaissance flute was largely of cylindrical bore, consisted of one or two pieces, and was without keys, the baroque flute consisted of three or more pieces, had one or more keys, and was for the most part of conical bore (that is, the diameter of the bore of the cylindrical head piece was greater than that of the foot piece, and the section or sections between had a bore of decreasing diameter from head to foot). The tapered bore not only improved the tuning of the upper (overblown) notes but also effectively flattened the scale; in compensation, the finger-holes were moved closer together. The six finger-holes, which are usually undercut in a gradually increasing width of diameter towards the interior of the instrument, are covered directly by the fingers. A seventh hole—rarely are there more on a baroque flute—is covered by a key, called the D♯ (or E♭) key.

The invention of the D♯ key on the foot piece around 1670 was an important achievement; it enabled the little finger of the right hand to push a lever (the key) to vent a hole out of reach of the finger and placed between the bottom end of the flute and the first hole. The newly bored hole produced d♯′.

---

[1] The most ambitious attempt to document the development of the baroque flute has been made by Jane Bowers, who published the results of her research in 'New Light on the Development of the Transverse Flute between about 1650 and about 1770', *Journal of the American Musical Instrument Society*, 3 (1977), 5–56. In addition to an examination of existing flutes, Ms Bowers makes detailed studies of iconographical materials which she attempts to date and relate to existing musical instruments. Philip Bate's book, *The Flute* (London: Ernest Benn Limited; New York: W. W. Norton, 1969, 1975) remains the most satisfying general book on the flute, distinguished by Bate's first-hand knowledge of historical instruments, his scientific background, and his talents as a writer. Another valuable short study is by Edward R. Reilly in *Quantz and His* Versuch: *Three Studies* (New York: American Musicological Society, distributed by Galaxy Music Corp., 1971), 93–104.

The extant original baroque flutes generally have pitches that range from A=392 to about A=415. They tend to play most satisfactorily in the first two octaves, from d' to d''', although low-pitched and so-called 'd'amore' instruments have easily played third octaves because the bore tends to be narrow relative to the length of the instrument.

Origins of the Baroque Flute

The baroque flute had apparently been developed by about 1670. Quantz, writing in 1752, described this development as follows:

The French, by the addition of a key, were the first to make the instrument more serviceable than it had been previously among the Germans. The exact time when this improvement was made, and who its originator was, cannot be fixed with certainty, although I have spared no pains to discover reliable answers. In all probability the improvement was made less than a century ago; it was, no doubt, undertaken in France at the same time that the shawm was developed into the oboe, and the bombard into the bassoon.[2]

In fact, the baroque flute developed slightly later in the baroque era than other wind instruments. The baroque oboe had been developed in France by about 1660[3] and Michel de la Barre (*c*.1675–*c*.1744), writing a memoir in about 1740, stated that from the time that members of the Philidor and Hotteterre families perfected the oboe for concert use, 'the musettes were left to the shepherds, violins, recorders, theorbos and viols took their place, for the transverse flute did not come until later'.[4]

The first known example of the inclusion of a transverse flute in the baroque orchestra—and it is indubitably meant to be the one-keyed flute—appears in Lully's *Le Triomphe de l'Amour* (1681). The earliest known datable pictorial representation of the baroque flute is found in the engraved frontispiece to Marin Marais's *Pieces en trio*, published in Paris in 1692. The engraving shows a number of contemporary musical instruments: oboes, recorders, a bassoon, viol, violin, and two one-keyed transverse flutes not unlike the type of flute which bears the mark 'Hotteterre'. (See Fig. 6.) Thus, a date of *c*.1670–80 seems reasonable for establishing the first appearance of the three-piece conical

---

[2] J. J. Quantz, *On Playing the Flute*, ed. and trans. Edward R. Reilly (London: Faber & Faber, 1966; 2nd edn., 1985), 30.

[3] See Josef Marx, 'The Tone of the Baroque Oboe', *Galpin Society Journal*, 4 (1951) 11–12.

[4] 'Mémoire de M. de la Barre', in J.-G. Prod'homme, *Écrits de Musiciens* (Paris: Mercure de France, 1912), 244.

one-keyed transverse flute. However, is this scanty information enough to state with certainty that the baroque flute evolved first in France?[5]

Richard Haka

A few years ago, a one-keyed flute made by Richard Haka was discovered in a private collection in The Netherlands. (See Fig. 4.) This is an important discovery in the history of the flute because its existence opens up the possibility that the one-keyed baroque flute may have evolved in his workshop in Amsterdam rather than in the workshops of the French. At the very least, it suggests that there was an exchange of information between Holland and France by the pioneer woodwind-makers of the baroque era.

Haka was born in London in 1646 and died in Amsterdam in 1705. He was thus of the generation of the father and uncles of the famous Jacques Hotteterre le Romain (1674–1763). Around 1652 he moved with his parents from England to Holland and began making woodwind instruments in Amsterdam around 1660.[6] Haka's surviving instruments, besides the one-keyed flute, include ten recorders, ten shawms and deutsche schalmei, six oboes, two tenor oboes, and one bassoon.[7] The fact that Haka made both shawms and oboes shows his position as one who bridged the Renaissance and the baroque period in instrument-making.

The surviving Haka flute is unusually low-pitched, playing at between b and bb at modern pitch (but not low enough to be a true flute d'amour, which is defined as being pitched in a, a minor third below the concert flute). It is made of boxwood and consists of three sections: head, middle, and foot. The head piece bulges near its lower end to form a tenon and socket joint with the middle piece. Six tone holes are found on the middle piece. A seventh tone hole, located on the foot piece, is closed by a key. The bore is conical, tapering from

---

[5] Nancy Toff, on p. 16 of *The Development of the Modern Flute* (New York: Taplinger, 1979), has stated (without giving sources for her information), 'The principal figure in the late seventeenth century remodeling of the flute was Jacques Hotteterre le Romain (ca. 1680–ca. 1761), one of a prominent family of musicians and instrument makers. His major contribution, which is generally dated about 1660, was the construction of the first one-keyed flute.' In *The Flute Book* (New York: Charles Scribner's Sons, 1985), Ms Toff states (p. 43): 'Jacques Hotteterre le Romain (1674–1763), a member of a distinguished family of French instrument makers, was the principal figure in the redesign of the baroque flute. His major contribution, the addition of the D♯ key, is generally dated about 1660.' Again, she does not give sources for this statement, nor does she explain how Jacques Hotteterre could have invented something years before he was born.

[6] For further biographical information about Haka, see Rob van Acht, 'Dutch Wind-Instrument Makers from 1670 to 1820', *Galpin Society Journal*, 41 (1988), 83–101, and William Waterhouse, 'A Newly Discovered 17th-Century Bassoon by Haka', *Early Music*, 16: 3 (1988), 407–10.

[7] Phillip T. Young, *Twenty-five Hundred Historical Woodwind Instruments* (New York: Pendragon Press, 1982), 62–3. Van Acht, 'Dutch Wind-Instrument Makers', 89, lists 12 recorders, 1 traverso, 7 oboes, 1 bassoon, and 9 'others'.

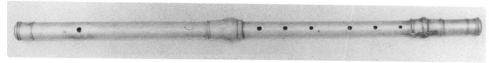

FIG. 4. One-keyed flute by Richard Haka. Private collection, The Netherlands.
Photo courtesy of Friedrich von Huene

FIG. 5. Two-piece keyless cylindrical flute by Lissieu. Kunsthistorisches Museum,
Vienna. Photo courtesy of Friedrich von Huene

the head to the foot. This flute shows strong similarities to a cylindrical two-piece keyless flute marked 'Lissieu' now in the Kunsthistorisches Museum in Vienna. (See Fig. 5.)[8] Jane Bowers has proposed that the Lissieu flute is a transitional instrument dating to 'about 1660–1675(?)' on the basis of Lissieu having already been established for some years by 1672 in Lyons as a maker of musettes and other wind instruments.[9] A comparison between the Lissieu and Haka flutes reveals major similarities in design, especially in the location of the embouchure hole in the head piece, the length of the head piece, the shape of the bulge containing the tenon and socket joint which joins the head piece to the middle piece, the turnings at the extreme ends of the instrument, and the relative location of the six finger holes. On the basis of such a visual comparison, it would seem possible that Haka may have been familiar with the Lissieu-type cylindrical flute (which by definition is still a Renaissance flute) and may have based his one-keyed, three-piece conical flute upon that design. Further research into Haka and Lissieu would seem to be in order at this time.

Even though Quantz, writing in 1752, speculated on the French as being the originators of the one-keyed flute, by his own admission he could not fix this with certainty. His speculation may have been wrong. Communication between France and the Prussian Court where Quantz was employed was close. Developments regarding the flute in Amsterdam may have had less chance to be brought to the attention of the Prussian Court.

---

[8] The Lissieu flute, in an unrestored state, is illustrated in Anthony Baines, *European and American Musical Instruments* (New York: The Viking Press, 1966), plate 458.
[9] Bowers, 'New Light on the Development of the Transverse Flute', 8–9.

The Hotteterre Family

In France, several generations of members of the Hotteterre family were involved in making and playing woodwinds. Until early in the seventeenth century the family had lived in or near La Couture-Boussey in Normandy, where wood-turning was practised. Moving to Paris, the various members of the family established themselves throughout the seventeenth century and into the eighteenth century as outstanding woodwind-instrument-makers and court musicians. Among those who excelled as makers were Jean Hotteterre and his nephew with the same name; Jean's son, Martin; Nicolas (l'aîné) and his brothers Louis and Nicolas (le jeune, le cadet), and Martin's son, Jacques ('le Romain'). Hotteterre marks also appear on various recorders and oboes, and contemporary accounts speak of their musettes, flageolets, and crumhorns.

If there were ever any transitional flutes in France between the keyless, cylindrical Renaissance flute and the elegant three-piece conical one-keyed flutes marked 'Hotteterre', none has survived (except for the Lissieu instrument). Three surviving flutes with the Hotteterre anchor stamp (now in museums in St Petersburg, Berlin, and Graz, respectively) are of superbly elegant proportions and design, as shown by the example in Fig. 6. It is not known which member of the Hotteterre family made these instruments; however, since the Berlin and St Petersburg instruments are so similar to the instrument which is illustrated in the *Principes de la flute traversiere* (1707) by Jacques Hotteterre le Romain, it has been assumed by many (without proof) that these instruments were made by Jacques Hotteterre.

The Hotteterre flutes in Berlin and St Petersburg are distinguished by a long ball-ended finial to cap the end of the head piece, a symmetrical centre ferrule joining together the head and middle pieces, and an ovoid foot piece. The ebony Hotteterre flute in Graz is similar except that the end finial is shorter and less rounded. The pitch of the Hotteterre flutes in Berlin and St Petersburg is about A=400, slightly less than one whole tone below modern pitch. The pitch of the Graz instrument is about A=392. The mellowness and richness of

FIG. 6.   Flute by Hotteterre. State Institute for Theatre, Music, and Cinematography, St Petersburg. Photo courtesy of Friedrich von Huene

tone of these instruments—especially in the low register—is startling to anyone who plays them or good replicas for the first time.

Other Makers of the Three-Piece Baroque Flute

Other French flute-makers of this period include Jean-Jacques Rippert, a maker named Naust, and another known by the name of Chevalier. Flutes by these makers incorporate modified designs of the Hotteterre style but continue the same tonal and pitch characteristics. (See Fig. 7, 8, and 9.) The dates of these instruments can only be attributed approximately; however, contemporary pictorial evidence suggests a dating of about 1680 to about 1715.

Three-piece conical baroque flutes were also crafted by distinguished makers in Germany and England. Jacob Denner (1681–1735), a member of a famous Nuremberg family of woodwind-instrument-makers, is known to have made both three-piece and four-piece flutes. Fig. 10 illustrates a rare ivory flute by Denner recently acquired by the Germanisches Nationalmuseum in Nuremberg. It is of special interest because, in addition to a foot piece to d′, it also has an alternate foot piece to low c′. Quantz wrote about such a flute:

About thirty years ago some persons tried to add yet another note, namely C, to the low register of the flute. To this end they lengthened the foot as much as was required for a whole tone, and, in order to have the C sharp, added another key. Since this seems to have been detrimental to the true intonation of the flute as well as its tone, the pretended improvement was not widely accepted and disappeared.[10]

The Denner flute at Nuremberg does not have a C♯ hole or key, such as Quantz described. Nevertheless, Quantz's date of about thirty years before 1752 (the date of his treatise) seems correct for the Denner flute. (A date of 1710 is marked on the flute; like dates on many old violins, however, this should be accepted with caution.) The instrument has a dark, well-focused sound and plays at about A=413. The fish-tail touch-piece of the low c′ key is of considerable interest, since, given the d♯′ key, the flute must be played right-handed. A fish-tail touch-piece can be justified only if the flute were to be played either right- or left-handed.

In England, three-piece baroque flutes were made by the great French-born craftsman, Peter Bressan (1663–1731). Bressan had been baptized Pierre Jaillard, but after emigrating to England in 1688 he began to use a more Anglicized name. The Bressan flute in the Dayton C. Miller Collection in

---

[10] Quantz, *On Playing the Flute*, 34

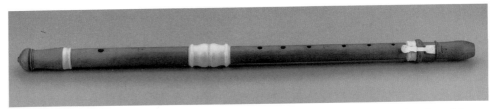

FIG. 7.   Flute by Chevalier. Museum of Fine Arts, Boston, Leslie Lindsey Mason
Collection, formerly the Galpin Collection; gift of William Lindsey. (No. 17.1846)

FIG. 8.   Flute by Jean-Jacques Rippert. Musée Engadin, St Moritz. Photo courtesy
of Friedrich von Huene

FIG. 9.   Flute by Jean-Jacques Rippert. Glasgow Museums and Art Galleries.
(Reg. No. '42-68ak)

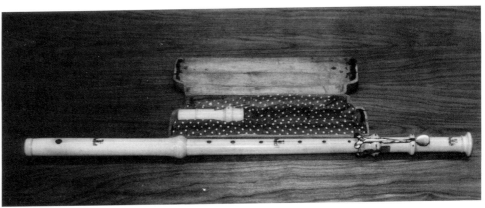

FIG. 10.   Flute by Jacob Denner, with two foot pieces. Germanisches Nationalmuseum, Nuremberg. Photo courtesy of Friedrich von Huene

FIG. 11. Flute by Peter Bressan. Dayton C. Miller Collection, Library of Congress, Washington, DC

Washington (Fig. 11) shows how Bressan took the basic Hotteterre design, and modified the ivory end cap on the head piece, redesigned the foot piece, but retained the symmetrical design of the centre ferrule. Bressan was probably one of the first flute craftsmen to make a four-piece traverso, a beautiful example of which may be seen at the Victoria and Albert Museum in London. Before discussing that instrument and other four-piece baroque flutes, let us first consider why the three-piece flute became a four-piece instrument, and when.

The Four-Piece Baroque Flute

Pitches varied widely in the baroque era from one place to another. Even the same harpsichord could be tuned to one pitch one day, another pitch the next. This caused problems for traverso players, because it was not practical to have a different traverso for each pitch encountered. It is true that some pitch change could be achieved by slightly pulling out the head piece of a three-piece traverso, but the resulting increase in the bore diameter at the gap could upset the tuning of the instrument. Around 1722, according to Quantz, the middle piece into which the six finger-holes were cut was redesigned to consist of two separate pieces of three holes each.[11] By replacing the upper of these two pieces with alternative pieces of greater or lesser length, the pitch of the flute could be raised or lowered. A well-equipped traverso-player could therefore have one flute with two or more centre pieces (which the French call *corps de rechange*) to accommodate a number of different pitches within a range of about a semitone.[12] (See Figs. 12, 17, 18, and 32.)

   The earliest known dated four-piece baroque flute is an instrument by the French maker, Charles Bizey, in the Germanisches Nationalmuseum in

[11] Ibid. 31.
[12] There is no reason why the entire centre section of a 3-piece traverso could not have been replaced by another full centre piece of different length to achieve a different pitch. In fact, it is acoustically better than changing only the upper half containing three holes, because the correct proportions of the tone hole placement can be maintained throughout the entire instrument.

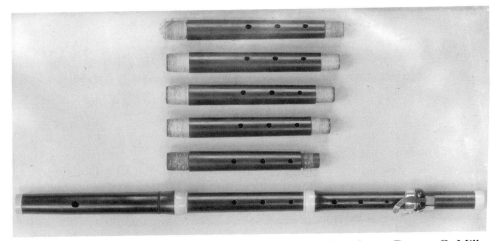

FIG. 12.   Flute by Johann Joachim Quantz, with *corps de rechange*. Dayton C. Miller
Collection, Library of Congress, Washington, DC

Nuremberg. It is stamped with the date 1736. The two surviving four-piece
Denner flutes (in museums in Brussels and Nuremberg, respectively) must pre-
date 1735, the date of Denner's death.[13] Likewise, since Bressan died in 1731,
his surviving four-piece traverso (illustrated in Fig. 13) must date before 1731.
The three-piece traverso continued to be played into the 1730s, and, even in
the light of Quantz's statement, cited above, which gives an approximate date of
1722 to the invention of the four-piece flute, relatively few four-piece instruments were actually made in the 1720s.[14] There was thus an overlap in the use
of three-piece and four-piece flutes of perhaps fifteen to twenty years, or longer.

Bressan's four-piece ebony traverso is one of the most famous and beautiful
of surviving baroque flutes. It is remarkable how Bressan not only made an
instrument which plays well—it is pitched at A=410, incidentally—but the
design of the instrument was quite unlike anything that had been done by his
flute-making predecessors.[15] Gone are the exuberantly curved finials and
ferrules of the Hotteterre-type flute. Instead, Bressan used flat silver ferrules

---

[13] A third 4-piece Denner flute—a small instrument presumably pitched a third or a fourth higher than
the ordinary flute—passed through Christie's salerooms in London on 16 Mar. 1988 (lot 208, illustrated).

[14] See Bowers, 'New Light on the Development of the Transverse Flute', 40, 55.

[15] A 4-piece ivory traverso marked 'Naust' which was sold at Sotheby's London (22 Nov. 1989, lot 66,
illustrated) shows unusually straight lines similar to the Victoria and Albert Museum's Bressan flute. Even
the key mount is like the V. & A.'s Bressan; called a slotted boss, this type of mount rarely appears on
baroque flutes and is more typically found on late classical flutes. Little is known about Naust, other than the
fact that several other surviving flutes are of three pieces and are in the style of Hotteterre's flutes.

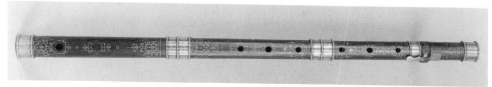

F IG . 1 3 . Four-piece flute by Peter Bressan. Photo courtesy of Board of Trustees, Victoria and Albert Museum, London

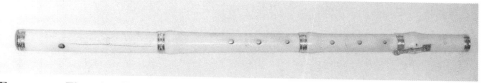

F IG . 1 4 . Flute by Thomas Stanesby, jun. Musée Instrumental du Conservatoire National Supérieur de Musique, Paris. Photo courtesy of Friedrich von Huene

and end cap, as if to avoid breaking the straight-line silhouette of the instrument, returning to something of the simplicity of the Renaissance flute. Against this controlled elegance, Bressan (or someone working for him) embedded silver filigree into the ebony, in marked contrast to the severity of the straight lines.

The standard of excellence which Bressan established as a maker was continued in England by Thomas Stanesby, jun. (1692–1754), whose *œuvre* includes over thirty-six surviving flutes, all of which are four-piece instruments. (See Fig. 14.) Generally of superb tone and excellent tuning, these instruments are sought after by collectors and are frequently copied by modern makers. Another baroque flute-maker active at about this time was J. J. Schuchart (*c.*1695–1758), who may have been born in Germany. (See Fig. 15.)

The Bressan four-piece flute and most of the surviving flutes by Stanesby, jun., are unusual among baroque flutes regarding the tenon and socket joint connecting the head piece to the middle piece: the tenon is on the head piece, the socket on the middle piece. (See Fig. 16.) Later English flutes (except some by Monzani) and all Continental baroque flutes have the socket on the head piece and the tenon on the upper middle piece. With the tenon on the upper middle piece, no ferrule is required on it. When extra upper middle pieces came into use, this was the cheapest and easiest way to produce them, since ferrules, made of ivory, metal, or horn, involved extra work in fitting them.

Many fine makers were busy on the Continent supplying four-piece baroque flutes in response to growing demand. In France, in addition to Bizey, such

FIG. 15. Flute by Johan Just Schuchart. Private collection. Photo courtesy of
Sotheby's, Inc.

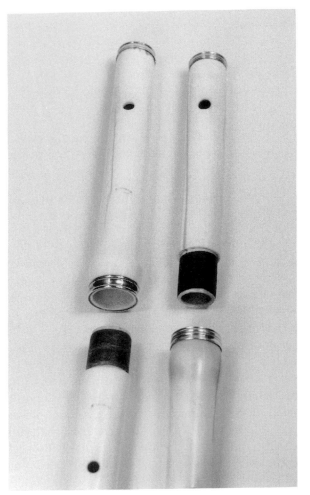

FIG. 16. Left, traverso with socket on head piece, tenon on middle piece. Right,
traverso with tenon on head piece, socket on middle piece. Photo courtesy of
Marcia Brown

flutes were made by Naust and by Thomas Lot, whose lengthy career flourished from 1734 to 1787.[16] In Brussels, outstanding instruments were made by Jean-Hyacinth-Joseph Rottenburgh (1672–1756) and his son, Godefried-Adrien-Joseph Rottenburgh (1709–90). The latter marked his instruments 'G. A. Rottenburgh' while the former used the mark 'I-H Rottenburgh'.

Many of the major German cities of the late baroque contained the workshops of noteworthy makers of woodwind instruments. In Leipzig, Johann Heinrich Eichentopf (1678–1769) and Johann Poerschman (1680–1757) both made a variety of wind instruments, including four-piece flutes. Poerschman is also important for being the teacher of Carl August Grenser (1720–1807), who moved to Dresden from Leipzig and opened his own workshop there in 1744. Grenser became one of the most important woodwind-makers of the eighteenth century. His flutes are not only of exceptional beauty and refinement but have excellent tonal characteristics as well. (See Fig. 17.) In Nuremberg, in addition to Jacob Denner, the Oberlender family made fine instruments. Four-piece flutes were made by J. W. Oberlender I (1681–1763) and his son, J. W. Oberlender II (1712–79). The latter joined the workshop of Jacob Denner in 1735, the year of Denner's death. In the town of Butzbach, two members of the Scherer family excelled at the making of wind instruments, Johannes Scherer, jun. (1664–1722) and his son, Georg Henrich Scherer (1703–78).[17] Thirty-eight of the surviving forty-one Scherer flutes are of ivory, and all of them are in four pieces. It seems likely that all of them were made by Georg Henrich; Johannes's death date of 1722 virtually precludes him from having made four-piece flutes. (See Fig. 18.) In Dresden for a short time and then in Berlin from 1741 until the end of his life, Quantz made and tuned flutes, many of which were produced for Frederick the Great of Prussia. Quantz's surviving flutes in the Library of Congress and in the collection of the late Robert Rosenbaum reveal that the pitch preference of Quantz was from A=392 to A=415; the *corps de rechange* cover that wide a range. Such a pitch-range was unusually low for mid-eighteenth-century European flutes. Quantz's flutes also favour a dark, mellow lower and middle register at the expense of the high register. This is not an accident but was a reasoned choice on the part of Quantz when he designed and made his instruments. The interior bore of the head piece of the Quantz flute in the Library of Congress has a diameter of 20 mm.—an unusually wide bore. In general, Quantz's flutes are atypical of mid-eighteenth-century flutes. In terms of tone quality and pitch, they are closer to the ideal of the French flute in use at the beginning of the eighteenth century.

---

[16] Dates provided by Tula Giannini, author of *Great Flute Makers of France: The Lot & Godfroy Families, 1650–1900* (London: Tony Bingham, 1993).

[17] See Phillip T. Young, 'The Scherers of Butzbach', *Galpin Society Journal*, 39 (1986), 112–24.

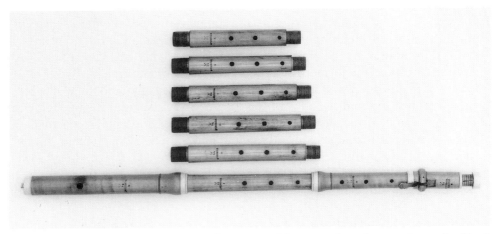

FIG. 17. Flute by Carl August Grenser, with *corps de rechange*. Augustin Ford Collection. Photo courtesy of Sotheby's, Inc.

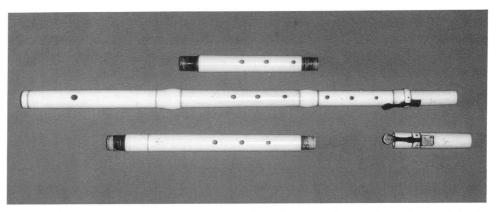

FIG. 18. Flute by Scherer with *corps de rechange* and two foot pieces. Musée Instrumental du Conservatoire Royal de Musique, Brussels. Photo courtesy of Friedrich von Huene

Mechanical Developments

Quantz's flutes were also mechanically different from other flutes of the same time. One of the most notable developments on his flutes is a second key on the foot piece designed to enable the player to distinguish between enharmonic notes such as E♭ and D♯. In the tuning systems generally used throughout most of the eighteenth century, the flat was played higher than its enharmonic sharp. Eb was sharper than D#. Quantz's system of fingering for the flute contains further enharmonic fingerings, four of which require the use of a second key operated by the little finger of the right hand. Quantz invented this second key (illustrated in Fig. 12) in 1726. It closes a second slightly smaller hole bored beside the Eb hole. By Quantz's own admission, the additional key never became popular, and only a few makers later in the century included it on some of their instruments, such as F. G. A. Kirst and Johann George Tromlitz.

In his autobiography, Quantz also claimed to have invented the tuning slide.[18] This is a second tenon and socket in the head piece, much thinner and longer than the other tenon which joins the head piece to the middle piece. In order to make pitch adjustments which are too minute to require changing the upper middle piece, the tuning slide may be pushed in or pulled out, thus lengthening or shortening the head piece. The tuning slide eventually became a common feature of flutes of the late eighteenth century and first half of the nineteenth.

Another mechanical development mentioned by Quantz is the screw cap and plug assembly in the head piece to facilitate the moving of the cork stopper. When the three-piece flute evolved into the four-piece instrument with alternate upper middle pieces, each resulting variation in flute length required a different placement of the cork. The shorter (and higher-pitched) the flute becomes, the further away from the embouchure hole the cork must be positioned. Likewise, the longer (and lower-pitched) the instrument, the closer the cork must be placed to the embouchure hole. While the cork was previously moved by pushing it with a rod or dowel, the screw cap and plug assembly enabled the cork to be moved simply by turning the end cap or pushing it in. Relatively few flutes had this device in the baroque era.

The *corps de rechange* also spurred the invention of the foot register, a telescoping section at the end of the foot piece. As the length of a flute is changed to enable the instrument to play at higher or lower pitches, the length of the foot piece should also be changed. The lower the pitch of the flute, the longer the foot piece should be. A flute by Scherer in the Brussels Musée Instrumental has two foot pieces, the longer of which should be used when the longest upper middle piece is used. (See Fig. 18.) Since it is impractical to have a separate foot piece for each alternate upper middle piece, the movable foot register was invented. In the Grenser flute illustrated in Fig. 17, the foot register is shown extended to its maximum length. Each line incised on the register is given a number which corresponds to the number on the alternative middle piece. Therefore, if the alternative piece marked '3' is used, the foot

---

[18] See Paul Nettl, *Forgotten Musicians* (New York: Philosophical Library, 1951), 318.

register should be extended to show the ring marked '3'. It is interesting to note that Quantz disapproved of this device.[19]

Alto Flutes, Bass Flutes, and Small Flutes

A number of surviving baroque flutes are found in sizes and pitches markedly different from the standard concert flute. These have names such as Quartflute, flute d'amour, and petite flute à l'octave. An F flute, pitched a minor third higher, is also known. Quantz writes that the low Quartflute is a fourth below and the flute d'amour a minor third below the ordinary flute, and the small Quartflute is a fourth higher. 'Of these, the flutes d'amour are still the best', Quantz writes, adding, 'At present, however, none approaches the regular transverse flute in trueness and beauty of tone.'[20]

A few exceptional examples of the flute d'amour survive, among them a three-piece flute by Naust now in the Musée Instrumental of the Paris Conservatoire and a fine ivory four-piece flute d'amour by Scherer in the Bate Collection in Oxford. Several flutes by Thomas Lot are bass flutes. The four-piece example in the Conservatoire des Arts et Métiers in Paris sounds a fourth below standard pitch.[21] Another celebrated low-pitched flute is a bass flute by Johannes Maria Anciutti, a maker who worked in Milan. This instrument, in Vienna's Kunsthistorisches Museum and dated 1739, is remarkable for the U-shaped head piece and the raised tone holes, all designed to facilitate the playing of this large instrument.[22]

Only a small quantity of music was composed expressly for the flute d'amour.[23] A concerto in B♭ for flauto traverso d'amore and strings by Johann Melchior Molter is found in the Badische Landesbibliothek in Karlsruhe. Christoph Graupner composed a handful of concerted works for flute d'amour and strings, the autograph manuscripts of which are found in the Darmstadt library.

The octave flute—what we today call the piccolo—also existed in the baroque age. Michel Corrette wrote about it in his *Methode* for flute, published *c*.1740. He states that octave flutes are currently being made in Paris and 'make

---

[19] Quantz, *On Playing the Flute*, 33–4.
[20] Ibid. 34.
[21] Illustrated in Bowers, 'New Light on the Development of the Transverse Flute', 44.
[22] Illustrated in Young, *Twenty-five Hundred Historical Woodwind Instruments*, plate XII.
[23] The late Christopher Addington attempted to demonstrate that the flute d'amour was the standard French flute of the age of the Hotteterres and that 'most if not all of Bach's chamber music for the flute was written for this instrument'. (See Addington, 'In Search of the Baroque Flute', *Early Music*, 12: 1 (1984), and 'The Bach Flute', *Musical Quarterly*, 71: 3 (1985). Rather than developing his topics objectively, Addington selected pieces of information to support his notions, using pseudo-scientific devices such as charts to argue his thesis. He tried to make the exception into the norm.

a charming effect in the Tambourins and in the Concertos written expressly for flute. Look at those of Albinnoni [*sic*], Corrette, Nodeau [*sic*], Braun and Quantz.'[24] Jean Philippe Rameau scored the piccolo even before Corrette's book was published, including it in the *Air pour Zéphire* in his 1735 opera, *Les Indes galantes*.

Fifes have been made since the late Middle Ages and the Renaissance. Whereas the bores of piccolos are conical, those of fifes are virtually cylindrical and are narrower relative to the length of the instrument. Fifes are usually in one piece, rarely have keys, and are usually pitched in B♭ or in C (a sixth or a seventh above the ordinary flute). With their characteristically bright and piercing sound, fifes are intended primarily for military use. One of the groups of Louis XIV's *Grande Écurie* was a fife and drum corps.

[24] Michel Corrette, *Methode pour apprendre aisément à joüer de la Flute traversiere* (Paris: Boivin, *c.*1740), 11.

4

The Classical Flute

THE classical flute emerged gradually, almost imperceptibly, out of the baroque flute—this is a modern distinction—just as the classical style of music was a gradual development from the baroque style. Indeed, the traverso's development was a reflection of the changing musical styles of the eighteenth century.[1] As the thicker contrapuntal textures of the baroque orchestra were transformed into the lighter, more transparent textures of the classical orchestra, so the darker sounds of the baroque flute turned into the lighter, brighter sounds of the classical flute. The higher pitches, higher tessitura, and greater flexibility of the classical orchestra were mirrored in the higher pitches, tessitura, and flexibility of the classical flute.

So subtle was this change over a period of several decades that in many instances the same mid-century flute could function in both worlds. In general, however, the classical flute tended to be pitched at around A=425 to A=435 (although some were pitched as low as A=415 and others higher than A=440), and it tended to play more convincingly in the second and third octaves, sacrificing power in the lowest notes for more easily produced higher notes. Makers created instruments which satisfied the needs of players who, in turn, were responding to the demands of the music they played.

The term 'classical flute' does not always mean an instrument with multiple keys. One-keyed classical flutes, such as those shown in Figs. 20 and 24, continued to be made and played throughout the entire eighteenth century and well into the nineteenth. Mozart's Flute Concertos in D and G (1778) were very probably written for the one-keyed flute; indeed, they lie beautifully in the fingers of any skilled performer who plays them on the one-keyed classical flute. Beethoven's Serenade in D, Op. 25, for flute, violin, and viola (1801), although with a very high tessitura, is another classical piece which may be played as successfully on the one-keyed flute as on a multi-keyed instrument.

---

[1] For a discussion of why the transverse flute gained popularity over the recorder in the 18th century, see Jeremy Montagu, *The Flute* (Princes Risborough: Shire Publications, 1990), 4.

Notable Continental Makers of Classical Flutes

Thomas Lot, G. A. Rottenburgh, and Carl August Grenser are three outstanding makers already mentioned as baroque flute-makers whose respective life spans brought them into the classical period. Since Lot worked until 1787, Rottenburgh until 1790, and Grenser until 1807, they all made classical flutes, virtually all of them being with one key.

Other distinguished Continental makers whose classical flutes were apparently of one key exclusively include Johann August Crone (1727–1804), Christophe Delusse (fl. 1781–9), and Jeremias Schlegel (fl. 1780–92). Crone worked in the important musical city of Leipzig; his life there overlapped with J. S. Bach's by twenty-three years. In performing characteristics and in design, Crone's surviving flutes show baroque as well as classical influences.[2] (See Fig. 19.) Delusse, who worked in Paris, made a variety of woodwind instruments of fine craftsmanship and excellent tuning. His flute shown in Fig. 20 is pitched at A=415, which suggests that pitch in Paris in the 1780s continued to be lower than in most of the other European and English musical centres. Jeremias Schlegel worked in Basle and also produced a variety of different wind instruments. All three of these makers created instruments distinguished by flexibility, light sounds, and easily produced high registers.

Working at the same time in Milan was Carlo Palanca, who made flutes, oboes, and recorders. A boxwood flute by him in the Library of Congress has five upper middle pieces.

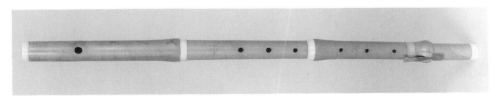

FIG. 19. Flute by Johann August Crone. Private collection. Photo courtesy of Stewart Pollens

[2] The difficulty of trying to label mid-century instruments as either 'baroque' or 'classical' is exemplified by the Crone flute illustrated in Fig. 19. On the one hand, this clean-lined instrument shows the design influence of the Leipzig maker, Johann Poerschman (1680–1757) whose life roughly corresponded with J. S. Bach's (1685–1750). (For an illustration of a Poerschman flute, specifically the one in the Institute of Theatre, Music, and Cinematography, St Petersburg, see Phillip T. Young, *The Look of Music* (Seattle: University of Washington Press, 1980), 89.) On the other hand, the shortest of the Crone flute's three upper middle pieces (numbered 1 to 3 and giving pitches of A=415, A=421, and A=439, respectively) and the flute's easily produced high register, are 'classical' characteristics. This instrument was used by the author to record Bach's E major Flute Sonata, BWV 1035, as part of his Arabesque recording of six Bach flute sonatas.

FIG. 20.   Flute by Christophe Delusse. Private collection. Photo courtesy of
Marcia Brown

Two of the most outstanding Continental makers who produced classical
flutes of from one to eight keys are F. G. A. Kirst (1750–1806) and Heinrich
Grenser (1764–1813). Kirst was apprenticed under C. A. Grenser in Dresden
and worked from 1770 to 1804 in Potsdam, eventually receiving an appointment
as flute-maker to Frederick the Great. His workshop was taken over by his
stepson, J. G. Freyer, who produced instruments under his own name as well
as in a partnership with the name of Freyer and Martin. Heinrich Grenser was
the nephew of C. A. Grenser, with whom he was apprenticed from 1779 to
1786 and from whom he eventually took over the workshop in 1796. He was an
extraordinarily prolific and versatile maker of all kinds of wind instruments:
flutes, oboes, clarinets, bassoons, basset-horns, and fagottini. At least thirty-five
of his flutes survive, including instruments of one, two, three, four, five, six,
seven, and eight keys. A Heinrich Grenser one-keyed boxwood flute with seven
interchangeable upper middle pieces is in the Smithsonian Institution in
Washington, DC, and is acknowledged to have some of the finest playing
characteristics of any one-keyed flute in a public collection in the United
States.[3]
     Johann George Tromlitz (1725–1805) is another German who was active in
Leipzig and whose influence is felt not so much through the flutes which he
made (of which very few examples are known) as through his published writings,
which explain, among other things, some of his inventions for the flute. (See
Chapters 7 and 8.) One of his few surviving flutes is shown in Fig. 21. A
detailed photograph (Fig. 22) shows one of Tromlitz's developments: placement
of the G♯ key on the lower middle piece rather than on the upper middle piece
(such as appears on the Kusder flute shown in Figs. 23 and 26). Placement of
the G♯ key had always been a problem because its proper location coincided
with a socket and tenon. Its placement on the upper middle piece necessitated
a short touch piece, which was awkward to use, and an excessively small tone
hole. Tromlitz's placement of it on the lower middle piece (with a corresponding
change in placement of the socket and tenon joint closer toward the head piece)
enabled the touch piece to be made longer and the tone hole to be larger.

---

[3] This Grenser instrument may be heard played by the author in a recording of Clementi's Sonata in G,
Op. 2 No. 3, on the Smithsonian Collection record entitled 'Music from the Age of Jefferson'.

Moreover, for a flute with *corps de rechange*, placement of the G♯ key on the lower middle piece eliminated the necessity of providing such a key on each interchangeable section (as is illustrated by the Gedney flute in Fig. 29).

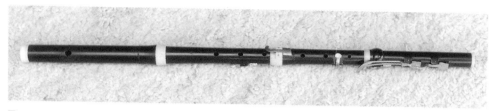

FIG. 21. Flute by Johann George Tromlitz. Private collection, Germany. Photo courtesy of Friedrich von Huene

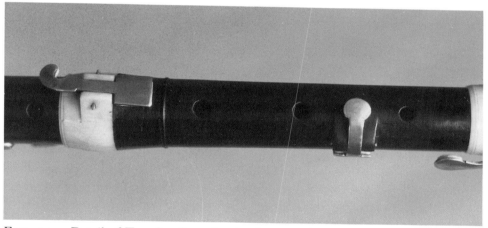

FIG. 22. Detail of Tromlitz flute showing lower middle piece with G♯ and F keys. Photo courtesy of Friedrich von Huene

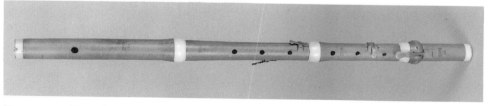

FIG. 23. Four-keyed flute by Henry Kusder. Private collection. Photo courtesy of Stewart Pollens

English Makers of Classical Flutes

In England the demand for flutes was so great in the classical age that literally dozens of flute-makers were kept busy meeting the demand. A separate book would have to be written to discuss in detail the complex world of English flute-making during this period (*c.*1750–*c.*1825), and much factual material remains to be discovered, sifted, and sorted. Often the instrument-making firms produced many different kinds of musical instruments, including pianos, violins, and other wind instruments, and some also published music. It is open to question if some of the firms actually made the flutes which they sold and stamped with their name. The makers were sometimes families (father and son, or brothers) and it is not always possible to distinguish which family member made a given instrument. Supplying flutes to a largely amateur market, the standard of workmanship of the English makers was frequently not very high (although there were some very fine makers creating excellent instruments at this time). Above all, England was at the forefront of mechanical change and development in the flute during this period.

Caleb Gedney (*c.*1728–*c.*1769) is important as a maker because he was apprenticed under Stanesby, jun., from 1743 to 1750 and, upon Stanesby's death in 1754, continued his operation at his premises. Few of Gedney's flutes appear to have survived, but one which does (Fig. 29) is important as proof that Gedney was one of the first to make flutes with multiple keys, as will be discussed later in this chapter.

Some of the best-known English makers were actually families of craftsmen, such as the Cahusacs. Thomas Cahusac the elder, active from *c.*1755 until his death in 1798, was probably the maker of most of the flutes which bear the Cahusac name. The best Cahusac flutes are of professional quality and are among the finest English flutes made in the classical era. His two sons, Thomas Cahusac, jun., and William Maurice Cahusac, also worked in the firm.

Among the most prolific of English makers was Richard Potter (1726–1806) and his son, William Henry Potter (1760–1848). The elder Potter had begun to produce flutes as early as *c.*1745. He was one of the pioneers in making flutes with multiple keys. (See Fig. 30.) William Henry Potter was apprenticed under his father and by 1801 the firm was called 'Potter and Son'.

Another English family of makers is the Milhouse family, the most important of whom was William (b. 1761). He was working in London by 1787 and enjoyed a long, successful career. His great reputation in his lifetime is verified by the many fine instruments he made, a large number of which still survive. A less well-known family of English makers is the Simpson family, which flourished from 1734 to 1795 over several generations. In addition to making flutes and violins, the Simpsons also published music.

A maker named Proser was active from 1777 to 1795. Theobald Boehm's first flute, played by him when he was about 15 years old, is a one-keyed instrument by Proser.[4] An instrument by Proser in the Bate Collection is exceptionally low in pitch for this period and therefore might be pre-1777. Other English makers of classical flutes are George Goulding, who was active from 1786 and who in 1798 went into partnership with Thomas D'Almaine and Phipps; Christopher Gerock, whose working dates are from 1804 to 1837; Longman and Broderip, a partnership which went into bankruptcy in 1798; Thomas Collier (active from *c*.1770 to 1791), who succeeded Charles Schuchart; John Hale, who succeeded Thomas Collier; James Wood, who flourished 1799–1808 and who got a patent for a tuning slide; John Cramer, not to be confused with the music publisher and piano-maker, J. B. Cramer; Herman Wrede, who worked 1810–49 and many of whose flutes are one-keyed; Thomas Prowse the elder; Thomas Key; George Miller; and John Willis.

Contintental-Born English Makers

Some of the most prolific producers of flutes in England at this time were men who had been born on the European continent and who made their careers in England. From Italy came Pietro Grassi Florio, Tebaldo Monzani, and Muzio Clementi. Florio (*c*.1730–95) enjoyed a very successful career as a performer in England. It has been suggested that Florio's instruments may have been made by John Hale.[5] Monzani (1762–1839) came to London in 1788 and became first flute at the King's Theatre, Haymarket. His instruments retained smaller tone holes rather than the larger ones espoused by Charles Nicholson. Clementi (1752–1832) was famous as a pianist and composer. He invested in various English musical instrument-manufacturing and music-publishing firms, all of which bore his name. It is uncertain to what extent the Clementi firm made the flutes it sold under his name.

Louis Drouet (1792–1873) was born in Amsterdam and lived in London 1815–19, during which time he produced multi-keyed flutes. His instruments, which can hardly be thought of as 'classical', were made by Cornelius Ward under his direction.[6]

---

[4] The pedigree of this flute is explained in Theobald Boehm, *The Flute and Flute-Playing*, trans. and annotated Dayton C. Miller (Cleveland, Oh.: Dayton C. Miller, 1922; repr. New York: Dover Publications, 1964), 3–5, illustrated in fig. 2.

[5] See the article on Florio in the *New Grove Dictionary of Musical Instruments*, i. 768, attributing this statement to Maurice Byrne.

[6] See Richard Shepherd Rockstro, *The Flute* (London: Rudall & Carte, 1890, 2nd ed., 1928; repr. London: Musica Rara, 1967), 285.

From Germany came the brothers George and John Jacob Astor, Valentin Metzler, and perhaps Henry Kusder. The Astor brothers started their business in London in 1782, manufacturing pianos and flutes. In 1797, John Jacob Astor left for North America where he became renowned as a fur trader, amassing an enormous fortune. George Astor continued the business in London until 1830 with such partners as Horwood and Gerock. Metzler established his firm in London in 1788 and became a successful maker of woodwind and brass instruments. Working on a much smaller scale than Metzler was Henry Kusder, about whom little is known. Since his flutes are stylistically similar to German classical flutes, and since his mark includes the double-headed Imperial eagle, it is sometimes suggested that Kusder came from Germany, although no actual proof of this has yet been found.[7] (See Fig. 23.) Kusder made flutes, oboes, clarinets, and bassoons of fine quality. He was also one of the first to make flutes with multiple keys, and for over two hundred years his name has been brought up from time to time as the possible inventor of three important keys in the history of the flute, namely, the F, G♯, and B♭ keys.

American Makers

Flute-making also found its way to America by the end of the eighteenth century. A maker who has been called 'the first important American maker of woodwind musical instruments'[8] is George Catlin (1778–1852). Born in Connecticut, he worked in Hartford from 1799 to about 1815 before moving to Philadelphia. It is not known under whom he was apprenticed. The flute in Fig. 24 is by Catlin working in association with Allyn Bacon between 1811 and 1814. This boxwood flute is clearly modelled after the English flutes of the time and compares favourably in playing quality with contemporary English flutes. Asa Hopkins (1779–1838), who was also born in Connecticut, was a clockmaker

FIG. 24.   Flute by Catlin and Bacon. Henry Ford Museum, Dearborn, Michigan.
Photo courtesy of Robert E. Eliason

---

[7] See the exhibition catalogue, *Historic Flutes from Private Collections* (New York: Metropolitan Museum of Art, July–Aug. 1986), item 5, p. 14.

[8] See Robert E. Eliason, 'George Catlin, Hartford Musical Instrument Maker', *Journal of the American Musical Instrument Society*, 8 and 9 (1982–3).

from 1810 to 1825. Thereafter, he began to make musical instruments, including flutes of from one to nine keys. Also born in Connecticut were the Meacham brothers, John (1785–1844) and Horace (1789–1861). At first they made instruments in Hartford, Connecticut. In 1810 or 1811 John moved to Albany, New York, soon followed by Horace. Their flutes all date from the Albany years and have from one to eight keys. A flute-maker who was active in New York from 1814 to 1831 is Edward Riley. It is not known where he was born; however, a one-keyed boxwood flute which was sold at auction in 1987 is stamped 'E. Riley, No. 8, Strand, London' and may be by the same maker before emigration to America.[9] Apprenticed to Riley in New York were both John Firth (himself born in England in 1789) and William Hall (1796–1874) who, singly, jointly, and also as Firth, Hall & Pond, became unusually productive makers of one-keyed and multi-keyed simple-system flutes. Their enterprise helped to supply the ever-growing demand from American amateurs for inexpensive flutes.

Mechanical Developments: the F, G♯, and B♭ Keys and additional keys on the foot piece

The F, G♯ and B♭ keys apparently first appeared in the 1760s, invented for reasons somewhat different from the invention of the D♯ key. They were designed to brighten the tonal characteristics and improve the intonation of three already-existing notes which formerly required 'forked' fingerings. The latter is a fingering with a sequence of open and closed holes on the flute such as the first and third hole closed ●○●|○○○ (for a♯″) or only the fifth hole open ●●●|●○● (to play f′ or f″). These forked fingerings tend to produce tones which are slightly veiled in tone quality and frequently too high in pitch. The player who reduces the breath or who manipulates the size, shape, velocity, and angle of the windstream in order to lower the pitch further veils the tone quality. It was probably in the 1760s that someone discovered that F, G♯, and B♭ could sound as strong and true in pitch as the rest of the scale if the forked fingerings used in playing them were replaced by fingerings utilizing keys that opened newly bored holes. These openings could be bored to the approximate size and location on the flute to produce a near-perfect F, G♯, and B♭. The B♭ key (Fig. 25) is operated by the thumb of the left hand. This thumb previously served no function for the flute-player other than to hold the instrument. The G♯ key (Fig. 26) is opened by the little finger of the left hand

---

[9] The auction took place at Sotheby's, London, 13 Nov. 1987, and the Riley flute, which is illustrated in the sale catalogue, is lot 172.

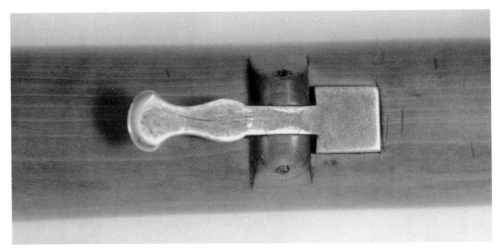

FIG. 25.   Detail of Kusder flute. B♭ key. Photo courtesy of Marcia Brown

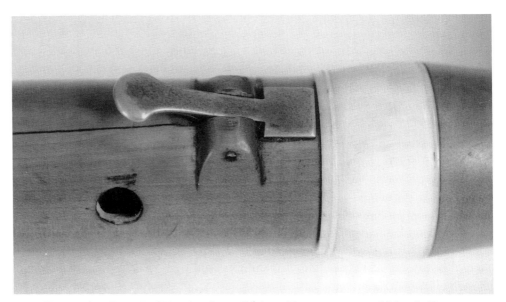

FIG. 26.   Detail of Kusder flute. G♯ key. Photo courtesy of Marcia Brown

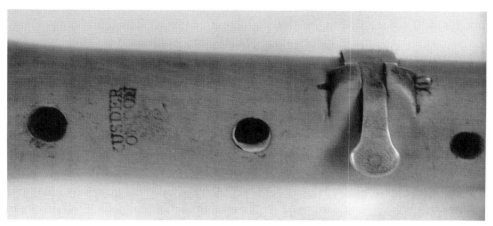

FIG. 27. Detail of Kusder flute. A view of the F key. Photo courtesy of Marcia Brown

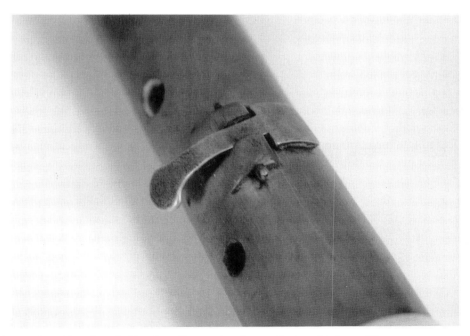

FIG. 28. Detail of Kusder flute. A view of the F key. Photo courtesy of Marcia Brown

(which also formerly had no function for a flute-player). The F key (Figs. 27 and 28) is operated by the fourth (ring) finger of the right hand.

Who could have been the inventor of these new keys? The evidence seems to indicate that it was someone working in England. In 1782 a book was published in Germany entitled *Bemerkungen über die Flöte* (Observations upon the Flute) by J. J. H. Ribock. He was a doctor and self-taught flautist who died in 1785 at the age of 42. Regarding the flute with the three new keys, he wrote, 'How old it actually is and who made it I cannot say with certainty. However, it appears to be no more than twenty years old and made either by Mr Tromlitz in Leipzig or by the instrument maker in London named Kusder, from whom I have seen no other flutes.'[10] This statement places the invention to a date around 1762. Tromlitz wrote prolifically about the flute, including commentary about his own inventions; he did not claim to have invented the F, G♯, and B♭ keys, however. By default, then, Kusder might be singled out as the inventor, although this is clearly speculative.

The B♭, G♯, and F keys on the Kusder flute shown in Fig. 23 appear so inconsequential that they are hardly noticeable. Indeed, at first glance the instrument looks like a one-keyed flute. The brass keys (shown in detail in Figs. 25, 26, 27, and 28) are simple, almost primitive, and of a very small size. The keys are highly similar to those which appear on the earliest known dated multi-keyed flute, a six-keyed instrument by Caleb Gedney, dated 1769 (shown in Fig. 29). Note that the Gedney flute has two additional keys on the foot piece to play c′ and c♯′. These two keys are 'open'; when the finger presses the touch piece, the key closes the hole. This action is the reverse of that of the B♭, G♯, F, and D♯ keys, which are 'closed', being simple levers which close the hole unless the finger presses the touch piece. Fig. 30 shows a flute by Richard Potter. This instrument is dated 1779 on the foot piece.[11] It shows strong similarities to the Kusder and Gedney flutes, although the F key is reversed, and the key work and overall instrument design seem to be more assured. If one compares these photographs, it does not seem impossible that the Kusder flute shown could date from the 1760s or that Kusder might have been the first to put these three keys on a flute. Conclusive evidence to prove this may never be found; however, there is no doubt that Kusder, Gedney, and Potter were among the very first to make four- or six-keyed flutes.

The standard classical four-keyed flute, therefore, consisted of the B♭, G♯, F, and D♯ keys. The standard six-keyed instrument of the same period consisted of these four keys plus the two keys on the foot piece to play c′ and

---

[10] J. J. H. Ribock, *Bemerkungen über die Flöte* (1782); facsimile ed. (Buren: Frits Knuf, 1980) (author's translation).

[11] Other multi-keyed Potter flutes exist stamped with the dates 1776, 1777, and 1778 respectively.

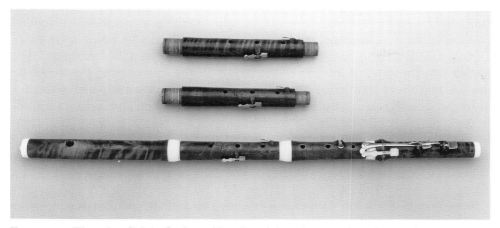

FIG. 29.   Flute by Caleb Gedney (dated 1769) with *corps de rechange*. Otis Norcross
Fund, Museum of Fine Arts, Boston

FIG. 30.   Six-keyed flute by Richard Potter (dated 1779). Augustin Ford Collection.
Photo courtesy of Sotheby's, Inc.

c♯, such as are found on the Gedney and Potter flutes. This was the flute which
Mozart had in mind when he wrote his Concerto for Flute and Harp, K. 299,
in 1778 in Paris, commissioned by the Duc de Guines, who had served in the
diplomatic corps in London. Mozart accommodated the six-keyed flute by
scoring a c′ in each of the three movements as well as one d♭′ in the first
movement. It is not difficult to imagine that the Duc de Guines brought back
to Paris from London one of the new Potter or Gedney flutes, since apparently
no multi-keyed flutes were being made in France at this time.

Although the extra keys discussed up to this point were in use frequently if
not generally in England in the 1780s and 1790s, the same was not true
elsewhere. The fingering charts which appear in treatises by Devienne,
Cambini, and Vanderhagen, all published in Paris in the last decade of the
eighteenth century, are for the one-keyed flute. (See Chapter 7.) Not until the

treatise of Hugot and Wunderlich of 1804 did a French tutor appear with fingering charts for the multi-keyed flute, which even then rejected the extended foot piece to c'. Devienne, in his introductory remarks to his flute tutor of *c.*1794, scoffs at the c' and c♯' keys which the English had added to their flutes, saying that those notes are out of the nature of the instrument. The proof he gives is that the acknowledged masters of the flute scarcely make use of them.

In fact, the one-keyed flute survived until the mid-nineteenth century. Flute-makers generally offered for sale a selection of flutes of one, four, six, and eight keys, and more. Of relevance to this development is the fact that the four-keyed flute may be played like a one-keyed flute by ignoring the three additional keys. When the four-keyed flute is changed into a six-keyed instrument by adding a foot piece with c' and c♯', it may still be played like a one-keyed flute (although one must pay attention to the use of the D♯ key, because some fingering changes are then required).

Additional Mechanical Developments

A number of new keys and various other inventions were applied to the standard four- and six-keyed flute later in the classical era. For the purposes of this book, we shall consider only those which the twentieth-century player is likely to encounter.[12]

The Long F Key

Since the finger of the right hand which operated the F key must also cover the sixth hole of the flute immediately to the right of the F key, the key becomes impractical to use if the preceding or following note requires the finger to cover the sixth hole. Sliding to and from the key is awkward. Tromlitz, in his book *Kurze Abhandlung vom Flötenspielen* (1786), writes about his invention of an alternative F key, usually called the long F key, which is operated by the little finger of the left hand. At first the long F key required a hole separate from the regular F hole. However, in another book, *Ueber die Flöten mit mehrern Klappen*, published in 1800, Tromlitz explains that he had modified the long F key to eliminate the duplicate F hole, the long key being made to engage the short F key directly. This duplicate F key, closing the same hole as the regular F key, may be seen on the Boehm and Greve flute in Fig. 31. The efficient design of

---

[12] For further reading concerning the many changes which occurred to the flute throughout its modern history, read Rockstro, *The Flute*, 2, pp. 131–401.

the long F key did not capture many advocates, however, as most of the simple-system flutes made after that time still retained the duplicate holes for F.

The C Key

With the invention of the keys for playing F, G♯, B♭, and D♯, every semitone of the scale on the flute had its own hole except c″ (and c‴). It was inevitable that a key should be invented to open and close such a hole. Ribock had invented such a key to be operated by the thumb of the left hand, but this proved to be impractical. W. H. Potter made a c″ key in line with the G♯ key and designed it to be played by the second finger of the left hand. This, too, failed to find favour.[13] The solution which became generally adopted was a long key played by the first finger of the right hand. (See Fig. 31.) Because this finger is kept so busy covering the fourth (F♯) hole of the flute, the use of the C key was very limited, being difficult to use in many fingering combinations. Its greatest success was as a trill key.[14]

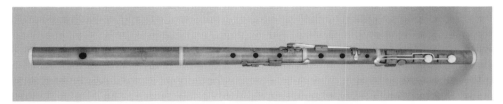

FIG. 31. Eight-keyed flute by Theobald Boehm and Rodol Greve. Collection of Helen and Charles Valenza. Photo courtesy of Stewart Pollens

---

[13] The earliest reference in English to this key is the 1806 edition of *Wragg's Improved Flute Preceptor.*

[14] Tebaldo Monzani wrote about the uses of the C♮ key in his *Flute Instructions*, 2nd ed. (London: The Author, *c.*1807), as follows: 'This key is intended to render the following Shakes, more brilliant, and easy. The many advantages accrueing from it, are such, as on the study of the following easy examples, must be obvious to every one. It is not here pretended to say, that the following Shakes have not been known before to others, but that they have never as yet been explained in any German Flute instructions: The Editor here vouches, that he was making various Experiments, since he himself has become a Manufacturer of German Flutes; and he is decidedly of opinion that the C♮ Shake Key is a very useful and pleasing acquisition to any Flute. This Key placed on the left hand side of the Flute as it has been and is now done cannot produce the same number of Shakes. By shaking the C♮ Key with the middle of the first Finger of the Right Hand, it will give a beautiful Shake to each of the following Notes. NB. Observe not shake it too fast, otherwise the shake will not be neat, or clear. Ex:

Pewter Plug and Salt-Spoon Keys

For most of the eighteenth century, keys consisted of a touch piece, a shank, and a metal flap faced with a thin layer of soft material such as leather to ensure an airtight closing where the flap comes in contact with the bored hole. For a flat key, a flat seating was cut around the bored hole. Towards the end of the eighteenth century and into the nineteenth, other types of keys were designed. As the flute acquired more keys, it became imperative that no air leakage should occur when a key was closed. Early attempts to create a new kind of key closing were by a German, Johann Friedrich Boie (1762–1809) and by an Englishman, Joseph Tacet.[15] The flat flap was replaced with a metal plug, a kind of cone-shaped valve (usually made of pewter) which came into contact with the bored hole. The hole itself was lined with silver. A similar invention was patented by Richard Potter in 1785.[16] Potter flutes of the nineteenth century commonly have pewter plug keys.

Another kind of key which appeared early in the nineteenth century is the so-called salt-spoon key. This key has a cupped or hemispherical shape, looking much like the back of a salt spoon. The hemisphere was stuffed with wool and covered with thin kid-leather. There were a number of different types of seatings for this key.

No modern makers of replicas are making flutes with pewter plug keys or salt-spoon keys. However, since they are frequently found on antique flutes from the first half of the nineteenth century, it is useful to be aware of their nature. As the interest in historical instruments grows, the day may come when instrument-makers will produce replicas of historical flutes with these types of keys. For the present, the classical flutes which are being copied all have flap-type keys.[17]

Metal-Lined Head Pieces

Since wood and ivory absorb moisture from the breath when the traverso is played, the head piece has a tendency to crack if preventive measures are not

---

[15] Rockstro, *The Flute*, 197.

[16] This was the first English patent for developments on the flute. Potter's patents included the keys for F, G♯, B♭, and D♯, the pewter plug key, the metal tuning slide in the head piece, the screw-cork with graduated, numbered lines, and the foot register. The slide, screw-cap, and foot register had a co-ordinated numbering system to ensure that the player made each corresponding adjustment correctly. For the most part, Potter's developments were not original, but the patent introduced the tuning slide and screw cork to England and brought together a number of important features.

[17] For further reading about keys on flutes, see Philip Bate, *The Flute* (London: Ernest Benn, 1969; New York: W. W. Norton, 1969), 214–28 and Rockstro, *The Flute*, 192–204.

taken, such as frequent swabbing. Another solution to this problem is to line the head piece with metal, since metal is not affected by moisture. Experiments with lined head pieces first occurred around the middle of the eighteenth century. Quantz mentions it in his 1752 treatise: 'Anyone who wishes to make the tone of the flute shrill, rude, and disagreeable can have it cased with brass, as some have tried.'[18] While lined head pieces are rare in eighteenth-century flutes, they are very common in wooden and ivory flutes throughout most of the nineteenth century. Rockstro, writing in 1890, states that all the English flute-makers, and most of the performers, had favoured metal-lined head pieces 'for the last seventy or eighty years'.[19] They were not generally adopted in France, although Drouet was an advocate, as was Fürstenau in Germany. The purpose of a lined head piece was threefold. First, it was meant to increase the brightness and power of the tone. This occurred at the expense of a certain warmth and sweetness of tone. Secondly, the tuning slide required at least a partially lined head. The third purpose was to prevent cracking from moisture. Although this may have been accomplished in the first years of use of any flute with a lined head, the ensuing one to two hundred years have taken their toll. For while the metal lining has remained rigid, the outer wood or ivory has slowly dried and shrunk. As the outer part has been unable to force the metal lining to shrink similarly, the result has been cracked head pieces by the hundreds if not thousands. All makers today model their replicas after original classical instruments with unlined head pieces, and modern players generally prefer their sweet, yielding sound. This may change in time as the early-music movement explores the nineteenth century with the same spirit and élan that it has explored earlier centuries.

Charles Nicholson and the Advent of the Romantic Flute

One of the most celebrated flautists of the early nineteenth century in England was Charles Nicholson (1795–1837), who was renowned for his big sound and bravura style. He played and endorsed flutes with big sounds made possible by large tone holes and large embouchure holes, and the head pieces were lined with metal. He marketed his design of instrument through other producers, such as Clementi & Co., Astor, and Potter, who inscribed them 'C. Nicholson's Improved'. Other English makers followed suit, or at least offered flutes with a choice of large, medium, or small holes. The French, meanwhile, still preferred

---

[18] J. J. Quantz, *On Playing the Flute*, ed. and trans. Edward R. Reilly (London: Faber & Faber, 1966; 2nd edn., 1985), 35.
[19] Rockstro, *The Flute*, 143.

the smaller tone holes, and the Germans responded to the new fashion from England to some degree.

The classical flute really came to an end when embouchures and finger-holes were enlarged in an effort to make bigger and brighter sounds. The nineteenth century brought the flute out of the drawing room into the concert hall. The orchestra was rapidly growing in size. The patronage of the arts was no longer the exclusive privilege of the aristocracy and the Church. The revolutionary age brought a broader base of support to the arts. The design of the flute had to be altered to produce a larger sound not only to project in the new, larger concert halls but also to hold its own in the expanding orchestra. A new generation of flute-makers left the classical flute behind and made flutes to play the music which we today call Romantic. In England, the partnership of George Rudall and John Mitchell Rose made outstanding large-hole flutes (as well as small-hole). In France, Clair Godfroy made exquisite flutes of both the simple system and, later, Boehm's system. Claude Laurent fashioned exotic and beautiful flutes from crystal or glass. (See Fig. 33.) Stephan Koch (1772–1828) made flutes with extended foot pieces to satisfy the demands of the Viennese who fancied playing below the normal lower range of the instrument.[20] In Berlin, Griessling and Schlott (founded in 1802) made a wide variety of instruments. And in Munich a young maker named Theobald Boehm, in association with Rodol Greve, around 1830 was making simple-system flutes as in Fig. 31. In the course of a few years, Boehm would transform the flute into an almost completely different instrument, reconceived and reconsidered from inside and out, top to bottom. The Boehm-system flute was imminent.[21]

---

[20] Stephen Preston plays such a Koch instrument.
[21] For additional discussion of large-hole versus small-hole flutes, see Peter H. Bloom, 'Observations on the Advantageous Use of the "Eight-Key" Flute', *Flutist Quarterly*, 11: 1 (1985), 18–25.

5
Buying an Instrument

THE acquisition of a good instrument is an important and necessary step in undertaking the study of the traverso. No single instrument will play everything equally well; experienced players generally have a variety of instruments for use as the nature of the music requires one playing quality or another. A typical collection of a professional player might include a three-piece French baroque instrument of the Hotteterre type, pitched at A=392; a four-piece baroque flute suitable for Bach and Handel, modelled after originals by Bressan, Stanesby, jun., or Scherer, with a pitch of about A=415; and a classical flute of from one to eight keys based upon original designs by Heinrich Grenser, Kirst, or Tromlitz, playing at a pitch of around A=430 and suitable for Haydn, Mozart, and Beethoven. Some of the replicas of mid-eighteenth-century instruments by makers such as C. A. Grenser or Rottenburgh can serve to play music of both the baroque and classical eras; in this case, modern makers provide *corps de rechange* to enable the instrument to play at different pitches, as required.

Tone and Sound

One of the most important characteristics to consider when buying a traverso is its tone or sound. No two instruments sound exactly alike, and players frequently have widely differing opinions about what constitutes a good sound. There are many factors which contribute to the sound of any given traverso, among which are embouchure size and shape, interior dimensions of the bore, and type of material from which the instrument is made. Generally speaking, the smaller the embouchure hole, the more focused is the sound; the larger the hole, the louder the sound.

Materials

While the size and shape of the embouchure hole greatly determine the quality and character of sound of an instrument, the material of which the traverso is made also significantly affects the sound. It is difficult to characterize sound in words; however, in general, the greater the specific density of the material, the denser the sound. Friedrich von Huene has calculated the following table of relative densities:

Ivory: about 2.00
Grenadilla: 1.35
Ebony: 1.3
Boxwood: 1.25
Rosewood: 0.8 to 1.0
Pearwood: 0.8

These materials, as well as glass and porcelain, were used in the baroque and classical periods for making transverse flutes. End caps and ferrules were fashioned from ivory, horn, bone, brass, gold, or silver, and the keys were made of brass, silver, or (rarely) goldplate.

Ivory instruments tend to have a more focused sound than wooden instruments, with a slightly hard-edged quality and perhaps less tonal flexibility than wood. Ivory was frequently used in the baroque and classical eras for the finest instruments. In the Soviet Union, mammoth tusks have been used for ivory in some baroque flutes made recently.

Boxwood is yellowish in colour, but sometimes it is stained to a dark brown. It generally offers a pleasantly 'woody' sound with a certain flexibility and character. There are two varieties of boxwood. Turkish boxwood was used most frequently for making transverse flutes in the baroque and classical ages. It is now extremely rare, so most boxwood used for making transverse flutes in America now comes from Venezuela and is called zapatero. It is somewhat less dense and has less oil content than Turkish boxwood.

Ebony is a strikingly beautiful dark wood which, when polished, takes a satin-like finish. It gives a mellow, warm sound which is perhaps somewhat lacking in 'bite' or 'edge'. It was the material preferred by Quantz for his wooden flutes.[1]

Grenadilla was rarely used for original baroque or classical flutes; however, it is now sometimes used by modern makers as a substitute for ebony. Its toughness and durability are desirable attributes, although perhaps it lacks the tonal suaveness and elegance of ebony.

Rosewood from Brazil was rarely used in the eighteenth century—Delusse is one who did—and only occasionally in the early nineteenth century by such American makers as Catlin, Meacham, and Asa Hopkins. It has a 'woody' tone quality, although less dense than the sound produced by grenadilla, ebony, or boxwood.

---

[1] J. J. Quantz, *On Playing the Flute*, ed. and trans. Edward R. Reilly (London: Faber & Faber, 1966; 2nd edn., 1985), 34–5.

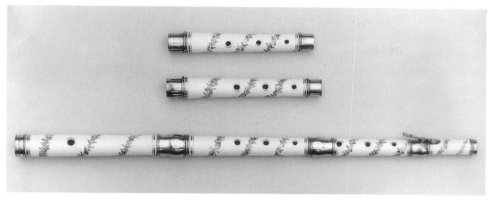

FIG. 32. Anonymous south German porcelain flute, mid-18th cent. with *corps de rechange*. Metropolitan Museum of Art, New York, gift of Thornton Wilson, 1943, in memory of Florence Ellsworth Wilson (43.34. a–g)

FIG. 33. Six-keyed glass flute by Claude Laurent (dated 1825). Augustin Ford Collection. Photo courtesy of Sotheby's Inc.

Pearwood is also rarely encountered in eighteenth-century flutes. It is a brown wood which expands and shrinks quickly in reaction to moisture from humidity or breath.

Porcelain and glass give a bright, clear, ringing sound and have no apparent pitch reactions to atmospheric change. The hardness of these materials gives a tone which is somewhat unyielding. A rare porcelain flute is shown in Fig. 32. The most frequently encountered glass flutes were made by Claude Laurent (fl. 1806–57), whose patent is dated 1806. (See Fig. 33.)

Condition, Pitch, and Other Considerations

An instrument under consideration for purchase should be carefully inspected for overall condition, since condition affects its performance and its value. A poorly fitted cork stopper, loose-fitting tenons, cracks, and keys which fail to cover holes properly can all contribute to leakage, adversely affecting the sound. Warpage rarely affects the tone, tuning, or volume of sound of a flute, but the visual peculiarity of it reduces the instrument's saleroom value. Some negative aspects of condition may be corrected, but others (such as a mutilated embouchure hole) cannot ever be restored to their original condition.[2] Further discussion of repairs is found in Chapter 6.

Pitch, too, affects the overall sound of an instrument. In general, the lower the pitch, the darker and richer the sound; the higher the pitch, the lighter the sound. In buying an instrument, one should ascertain at what pitch or pitches it plays. This should agree with the general pitch range of the era and country of origin. If an antique flute from the mid-eighteenth century plays at A=440, it is frequently a clue that the instrument may have been shortened in length in more recent times. It is sometimes possible to see where the instrument has been cut by comparing the colour of wood under the various thread wrappings on the tenons. If one tenon appears to have been lathed more recently than the others, then this may confirm one's suspicions about the length having been shortened.

Tuning and temperament are also factors to consider in buying an instrument. Throughout the greater part of the eighteenth century, flutes were generally not tuned to equal temperament. Ideally, one should develop an ear for distinguishing the various tuning systems which were used in the baroque and classical eras. Modern replica flutes which ignore the historical (unequal) tunings in favour of equal temperament are not able to offer the subtle variations of colour and expression which unequally tempered instruments offer. A detailed discussion of tuning and temperament is found in Chapter 10.

When ordering a new traverso or buying a second-hand one, the type of sealant in the bore should be noted. Two types are possible: oiled or varnished. Almost all players today prefer the tone quality provided by an oiled bore as well as the advantage inherent in being able to control the degree of porosity of the wood by the amount and frequency of oiling. Varnished bores, identifiable by a shiny finish, are permanently sealed. While providing maximum resistance to moisture, the resulting brighter sound loses some of its characteristic 'woody' quality. Instruments with varnished bores may be advantageous for educational or institutional use where players may be neglectful about oiling the bore or swabbing moisture from it. See Chapter 6 for further information about oiling.

The tenons of most wooden or ivory flutes are wrapped with thread. Occasionally flutes from the nineteenth century and modern replicas have cork wrappings. A cork-covered tenon will not inhibit the expansion or contraction

---

[2] An embouchure which has been damaged or enlarged may be 'bushed' and redrilled, but this is to be recommended only for rescuing an otherwise excellent instrument.

of the wood or ivory caused by changes in humidity and moisture from the breath. A thread-wound tenon will force all expansion inward, thereby slightly changing the diameter of the bore and ultimately altering the tuning of the instrument. However, cork lacks the advantage which thread gives in allowing small amounts to be added to or subtracted from the wrappings on the tenon to assure a snug fit with the socket at all times. Cork is generally avoided on antique flutes because it seems less 'authentic'.

Antique or Replica?

In acquiring a first traverso, one must make the decision of whether to buy an antique or a modern replica (new or second-hand). Because the flute was so popular from the late seventeenth through the eighteenth and nineteenth centuries, large numbers of instruments were made. Although relatively few true baroque flutes survive today, many original classical instruments exist. There are advantages and disadvantages to be considered in acquiring either an antique or a replica.

Antiques

An antique traverso in good playing condition is a primary source of information about tone, pitch, and temperament. There is a special joy and pride in owning an instrument which has historical value and which can contribute to our knowledge of musical history. While most of the best-known baroque and classical flute-makers are represented among the replicas being made by our best modern makers, there are many fine original instruments which appear on the market by less well-known makers and in some instances by makers of whom no trace survives except for a single instrument.[3] Anonymous (unmarked) flutes of quality are not uncommon. The best antique flutes may also have a special tone quality which has not yet been duplicated by even the greatest modern makers. Perhaps the age of the wood or ivory contributes to this, and perhaps there are subtleties about flute-making which the modern makers have not yet discovered.

Another advantage in owning an antique traverso is economic: its value will probably increase over a period of time from the law of supply and demand. Like investing in fine art, autographs, or antique furniture, an investment in a fine antique traverso can be rewarding in terms of capital growth over the long term.

---

[3] Dr Nicholas Jackman, an accomplished English amateur, plays an excellent boxwood flute of *c.*1800 by Fassbender, a name which apparently has not yet appeared in any lists or indices.

However, there are disadvantages to owning or playing an antique instrument. Any antique instrument is inherently fragile. One must be especially careful to guard it against excessively quick changes in atmospheric conditions, which can cause cracks. Antiques are especially vulnerable to cracking in homes with central heating or from jet-age travel. Antiques (as well as modern replicas) should not be played continuously for long periods without being allowed to dry out. A cracked head piece on an antique may be repaired but it can never be returned to its original condition, whereas damage to a modern replica may be corrected, if not with a repair, then with a replacement piece from the maker.

Another disadvantage in buying antique flutes is that many of them have developed internal intonation problems. As an instrument is played over a long period of time, the dimensions of the bore of the instrument gradually change and the tuning of the instrument may be altered. How to attempt to alleviate this common problem is discussed in Chapter 6. Another negative factor in buying an antique flute is cost. While it is still possible to acquire a satisfactory classical instrument in the same price range as a top-quality modern replica, one would normally expect to pay from five to thirty times (or more) as much for an authentic antique in fine condition by an acknowledged master than for the same instrument made in replica by a modern maker.

In buying antiques, one must be alert for instruments which are fraudulently stamped. It is not unknown for an anonymous (unstamped) antique flute to have been branded falsely in more recent times with the name of a famous maker. An antique should be judged by its basic characteristics rather than by the maker's marks. The value of an instrument should be determined largely by how it plays and its condition. The greatest makers, such as Stanesby, jun., Bressan, and the Grensers, have achieved their reputations by the quality of the instruments which they have created.

Sources of Antique Flutes

The two principal sources of antique flutes are auction houses and dealers. London is unquestionably the world centre for both sources. Three internationally known auction houses hold regular musical instrument auctions in London.

Sotheby's usually holds two major sales of musical instruments each year, and many important wind instruments pass through their salerooms. The instruments are on public view for three days prior to each auction. However, if a prospective purchaser is in London when a musical instrument auction is not imminent, the musical instrument department will gladly show what is on hand. An appointment is necessary in this case, however. For those unable to come to London, it is possible to bid by mail or telephone. One may subscribe to the catalogues by mail or order individual catalogues. If one wishes to learn more about a specific instrument, one may ask for a condition report from Sotheby's via telex (through the nearest Sotheby office) or by phone or fax. In the catalogue descriptions, a maker listed as 'by' (such as 'by Stanesby, jun.') means that Sotheby's will guarantee the authenticity for five years. 'Ascribed to' is vaguer than 'by'. 'Attributed to' means, essentially, that Sotheby's does not agree with the maker's attribution. A fourth category, 'stamped', simply means that an instrument is stamped with a name, which may or may not be a forgery. Sotheby's New York, which has not had musical instrument auctions for a few years, searches for musical instruments in America and forwards them to London for auction. In purchasing at auction, it should be noted that a 10 per cent buyer's premium is added to the hammer price. In addition, VAT (value added tax) is applicable to the 10 per cent premium. If the purchase price of an instrument is less than £16,000, no export licence is needed. Licences are also required for exporting any object from the UK which is made of or includes, in part, material from endangered species. Flutes of ivory or with ivory mounts come under this category. Sotheby's is prepared to arrange shipping and to apply for the export licence, if needed, on behalf of the purchaser.

Christie's also offers musical instrument auctions several times per year on an operating basis similar to Sotheby's. A condition report of any instrument will be sent via telex, telephone, or fax, upon request. Instruments may be inspected privately before public exhibition, and bidding may be done by mail (or by telephone if the minimum bid is £10,000) as long as the prospective buyer has provided banking references. In addition to the regular auctions each year, Christie's also holds three or four 'Objects of Art' sales (which include musical instruments) at their South Kensington salerooms.

Phillips has ten musical instrument auctions per year. Their principal strength is string instruments; however, fine, rare woodwinds do occasionally appear on the auction block here. It is possible to preview items about a week before each sale. Bids through the mail are possible upon presentation of references.

Needless to say, buying an instrument at auction may be riskly. While it is occasionally possible to find a bargain, it is also possible to bid excessively for an item. Purchasing an instrument unseen is also risky. In spite of condition reports, no amount of description can reveal the tone quality or 'feel' of an antique instrument or its tuning or temperament. If one cannot personally play an instrument for which one is interested in bidding, one should arrange instead to have a trusted and knowledgeable friend try the instrument. Many instruments at auction are not in playing condition for minor reasons: the absence of an end cork or a loose-fitting tenon. Other instruments may fail to play well for major reasons, such as a crack or a damaged embouchure. One needs to weigh carefully to what extent the damage detracts from the value of the instrument and then bid accordingly.

An alternative to bidding at auction in the quest for an antique traverso is to buy from any one of the dealers who trade in such instruments. Buying from a dealer may be more expensive than buying at auction (since dealers frequently buy at auction and resell at a profit); however, this is not always necessarily true. There have been many instances of dealers in the fine arts and antiquities who have sold stock items at auction for prices higher than they had been offering them for sale prior to auction. As a guide, recent auction prices of selected musical instruments are usually mentioned in reports contained in the journal *Early Music*. Sales price lists of the musical instrument auctions held by the major auction houses are available by mail for a small fee or may be seen at their respective offices in London or New York. Prices of rare items, such as antique flutes, are relative. Today's high price may be tomorrow's bargain price. Part of the fun of looking for antiques is the surprise of finding a rare item in an unlikely place. Antique flutes keep surfacing, and a great treasure may be awaiting your discovery!

A selective list of important dealers of antique flutes is found in the Appendix.

Modern Replicas

The major alternative to buying an antique flute is to buy a new modern replica of a specific historic flute. There are now a few makers in the world producing high-quality instruments which compare favourably to the finest instruments of the baroque and classical eras. This is a very recent development; thirty years ago there were none.

Fine old violins command large sums of money partly because even outstanding modern replicas can scarcely begin to compare with them. Not only were the standards of violin-making very high in the baroque era, but the ageing of these instruments in the intervening centuries has darkened the sound. Such is not necessarily the case with antique flutes, however: they do not always improve with age. It is perhaps true that the greatest antique flutes may have tonal superiorities to the best modern replicas, but the degree of difference is not as much as generally exists between old and new string instruments.

What are some advantages of buying a modern replica over an antique? One may choose not only the modern maker but the prototype maker as well. Pitch or pitches may be specified as well as any special requirements in tuning or temperament. One may sometimes choose the type of wood from which the instrument is made, the type of sealant of the bore, and the type of wrappings on the tenons. One may select the number and pitches of the *corps de rechange* and, in some cases, whether or not to have a foot register. On classical flutes, one may select the number of keys if the maker offers such a choice. Budget-minded players may sometimes choose to forego ivory mounts for plastic, artificial ivory, or perhaps none (i.e. unmounted). Above all, the purchase price of a replica traverso is relatively reasonable. For such a modest investment, what other instrument offers the opportunity to play one of the most important instrumental repertoires from the baroque and classical periods?

There are some disadvantages in buying a modern replica. There is a possible decrease in value. In reselling an instrument, it may be necessary to take a financial loss. The same risk factor exists for antique flutes, of course, but in the past ten or twenty years, the increase in value of a good antique flute has far exceeded the increase in value (if any) of a good replica.

If the maker is not careful, the wood of a new replica may not be properly seasoned, and this may result in eventual warping. Antique flutes have generally done all of the warping that they are going to do.

Sound *per se*, even by the best contemporary makers of replicas, may be perceived in terms of the twentieth century. In creating a replica, the maker cannot entirely erase his or her experience with the sounds of our time. Moreover, there is always the temptation of modern makers to produce flutes with the kind of sound that they know their clients want, rather than the kind of sound which may be heard in playing the antique original which they are copying. We live in an age when there is premium on bigness of sound. There are many extant flutes from the past with small but exquisite sounds which no maker today is willing to copy because these instruments do not fulfil the expectations of today's buying market. Big sound is today's fad.

There is another faddish aspect to replica flutes. With such a wealth of flute sounds and historical styles from which to choose, there is a disappointing sameness to the replica flutes which are purchased by players. Three or four historic flutes have been copied over and over again by numerous makers, in response to popular demand. Just observe the many copies of the Berlin Hotteterre, of Barthold Kuijken's Rottenburgh, and of the Victoria and Albert Museum's Bressan, while other important flutes are largely ignored. As Stephen Preston has pointed out, the current popularity of Rottenburgh copies is 'a historical accident' since it is doubtful if Rottenburgh's instruments, as fine as they are, exercised much influence on the great European flautists or composers of the eighteenth century. Among the important makers whose instruments have not yet been replicated are Jakob Grundmann of Dresden, J. W. Oberlender II of Nuremberg, Kaspar Tauber of Vienna, Jeremias Schlegel of Basle, Christophe Delusse of Paris, and Caleb Gedney and Henry Kusder of London. It is a continuing challenge for makers and players alike to keep searching for instruments which will more faithfully recreate the musical masterworks of the Renaissance, baroque, and classical eras and to keep an open mind about the tuning and the tonal qualities which the originals present. It will be a pity if we lose the diversity that was so characteristic of the instruments made in the centuries previous to ours.

Problems in Making Replicas

No replica flute is perfect, and each one involves compromises and aesthetic judgements on the part of the maker. Indeed, dozens of decisions must be made in modelling a replica after an original. Slavish imitation of the measurements of an original will not necessarily produce a good replica, although a good copy is more likely to result from copying a good original than a poor one. The ideal replica should have the tonal and overall playing characteristics of the original. In terms of the tuning, success or failure is very much in the hands of the modern maker, since many originals today have faulty tuning and are at pitches which are currently not fashionable (such as A=410 or A=420). To convert an A=410 original into an A=415 replica involves considerable experimentation on the part of the modern maker.

Makers of Today

There are many makers of Renaissance, baroque, and classical flutes active in the world today. It is not the purpose of this book to list all of them. The truth is that there is a handful of makers whose position of pre-eminence is generally accepted; they will be discussed in some detail. It is interesting to note that most of them now work in the United States, although several were born on the European continent or in the United Kingdom and now spend the greater part of the year working in the United States.

The first post-war traverso-maker to copy historical models and to establish high standards of workmanship was Friedrich von Huene. He has made successful copies of important instruments by Hotteterre (St Petersburg, the original of which is shown in Fig. 6), Chevalier (Boston, the original in Fig. 7), Scherer (Brussels, the original shown in Fig. 18), Kirst (original in Berlin), and Quantz (Washington, original shown in Fig. 12). Other replicas which he has offered are by Denner, Eichentopf, Rippert, Naust, C. A. Grenser, Bressan, Rottenburgh, Haka, and classical flutes by Tromlitz and Heinrich Grenser. He also makes baroque and classical piccolos as well as Renaissance flutes. Von Huene has spent years studying historically significant flutes and has amassed a large collection of measurements, drawings, and photographs of many specific instruments. It will be interesting to see what other great flutes will be copied by von Huene in the years ahead.

A number of craftsmen have been trained in the von Huene workshop and have gone on to establish their own workshops. One of the most prominent of these is Thomas Prescott, an American-born maker who has an international reputation for making recorders as well as flutes. He was apprenticed under von Huene from 1973 to 1975. Even before he left the von Huene workshop, he had already commenced working under his own name as an independent maker. He is now making only one replica traverso, a copy of the C. A. Grenser flute in the Dayton C. Miller Collection at the Library of Congress in Washington. This replica has enjoyed great popularity as an all-purpose eighteenth-century instrument and has been used for numerous recordings.

In the duration of a few short years, Roderick Cameron has established his reputation as an important traverso-maker. Born in Scotland, he now lives and works most of the year in California. As a teenager, he began work as a toolmaker's apprentice at the Rolls Royce Company, where he served for seven years. He eventually earned a master's degree in mechanical engineering and in 1963 entered Cambridge University to earn a doctorate in engineering research. In about 1971 he began to consider making woodwinds. He did not serve an apprenticeship under any other woodwind-makers; instead, he devised his own methods and tooling. He started to make baroque flutes after moving to San Francisco in 1975 and now offers replicas of many historic instruments, including a copy of Barthold Kuijken's G. A. Rottenburgh flute, the Victoria and Albert Museum's Bressan, an ivory flute by Stanesby, jun., and a classical flute after models by Heinrich Grenser. In addition, he makes copies of instruments by Hotteterre, I. H. Rottenburgh, Naust, Scherer, Bizey, Cahusac, Palanca, and C. A. Grenser, as well as Renaissance flutes. He also offers a modified version of the plastic Aulos baroque flute for less than half the cost of one of his own replica flutes. He supplies an Aulos traverso with a bore which he re-reams to his specifications and to which he adds a new upper middle piece for playing at A=415 (in addition to the A=440 Aulos upper middle piece). The result is a budget-priced, well-tuned baroque flute with a good sound.[4]

Another gifted maker from the British Isles who now works and lives in America is Ardal Powell. Together with his wife, Catherine Folkers, he makes instruments under the joint name of Folkers & Powell. Powell studied at Magdalene College, Cambridge, and took a three-year course of music study under Barthold Kuijken at the Royal Conservatory in The Hague. Folkers

---

[4] Aulos also makes a plastic flauto traverso at A=415 based upon an original instrument of Stanesby, jun.

began her career as a traverso-maker as an apprentice in the workshop of
Thomas Prescott, at the same time earning a performance degree at the New
England Conservatory of Music in Boston. In 1978 she set up her own
independent shop and made baroque flutes for six years. In 1984 she became
curator of the Dayton C. Miller Collection in Washington, DC, but returned to
full-time flute-making a year later in partnership with Powell. Their very
intelligent and serious approach to flute-making has produced a wide range of
replicas of original flutes by Hotteterre, Quantz, the Rottenburghs, Thomas
Lot, Buehner & Keller, F. Boie, and Heinrich Grenser, as well as a piccolo by
an anonymous maker working in Dresden *c.*1760.

   With such esteemed makers as von Huene, Prescott, Cameron, Folkers, and
Powell working mostly in North America, one might wonder who are the
outstanding makers on the other side of the Atlantic. Rudolph Tutz of
Innsbruck, Austria, has a great reputation but remains somewhat inaccessible
to the English-speaking world. He is noted as a superb craftsman who prefers
to work together with the musician for whom he is making the instrument, as
exemplifed by his association with Barthold Kuijken. Tutz is reputed to be
capable of making almost anything his clients want, whether it be a clarinet or
an eight-keyed flute. He may have been the first modern craftsman to make a
replica of an eight-keyed flute.

   Another distinguished Continental maker is Dr A. Weemaels in Brussels.
Other noted makers include Alain Winkelman (Switzerland), Stefan Beck
(Berlin), and Claire Soubeyran (Paris). However, like Tutz and Weemaels, they
do not actively market their instruments in the British Isles or in North America,
and it is not easy to find information about them since they do not generally
advertise in the English-language early-music journals. As Lisa Beznosiuk once
observed, the makers on the Continent 'seem distant'. Perhaps this will change
in the next few years.[5]

   There are other dedicated makers in the world whose efforts deserve
recognition and whose work is being followed with interest, among them Sam
Murray in Ireland, Gerhard Kowalewsky in Germany, Brian Ackerman,
Douglas Norfolk, and Matthew Dart in England, Jean-Luc Boudreau and Jean-
François Beaudin in Canada, Felix Raudonikas in the Soviet Union, Andreas
Glatt in Belgium, and Robert Gilliam-Turner and Patrick Olwell in Virginia,
USA.

   First-time purchasers of a replica traverso should become acquainted with as
many instruments of the leading makers as possible to become familiar with the
standards of the profession. One may examine instruments by visiting the

---

[5] In her New York début recital in March 1991, Ms Beznosiuk used a traverso by Weemaels to perform
Bach's Partita in A Minor.

workshops of the foremost makers, although such a personal call inevitably takes them away from the workbench. One may also inspect instruments at the international early-music exhibitions which take place in Boston, London, Bruges, Utrecht, and elsewhere, as scheduled. Many of the leading makers attend, bringing with them representative examples of their work. Some also exhibit at the annual convention of the National Flute Association, held each August at a different location in North America. Most makers will also provide the name of the person nearest you who owns one of their instruments and who, in all probability, would be willing to allow you to examine it.

All of the major makers have descriptive price lists. Modest deposits are usually required at the time of placing an order. The better-known makers are sometimes months, even years, delayed in filling orders. If you are urgently in need of a new traverso, you may prefer to invest in a good instrument by a less well-known maker, or you may prefer to buy a used (second-hand) replica by a noted maker. Second-hand replicas may be found at some of the early-music shops. (Many shops also carry a limited supply of new replicas as well as the occasional antique flute.) Whether an antique or a modern replica, whether by a noted maker or by someone quite unknown, buying a traverso is always an exciting experience.

6

Care and Maintenance of the Instrument

ALL musical instruments need good care and maintenance, and the traverso is no exception. These wooden or ivory instruments are very different from the metal Boehm-system flute; while they are mechanically simple and do not usually need delicate adjustments, they do require special handling. Proper restoration of an antique traverso should bring the instrument up to maximum playing condition (if restoration is feasible) and, in the case of both antique and modern replica flutes, careful maintenance should keep them in good playing condition for an indefinite period of time. Moreover, there is a financial factor to be considered: an instrument in fine condition is worth more than a similar one in poor condition. Common sense tells us to conserve and preserve our assets.

When You Acquire an Antique

Many antique flutes need repairs when purchased. A traverso which may appear to be in fine condition will, upon closer inspection, frequently reveal carelessly done old repairs, hairline cracks, faulty or broken keys, ill-fitting tenons, and other matters which must be corrected if the instrument is to play well. Both antiques and replicas can also be out of tune with themselves. There are two different causes of this: poor design and deterioration of the instrument. As will be discussed later in this chapter, it is sometimes possible to improve tuning without compromising the instrument.

Some antiques are not worth attempting to restore. The cost of repair would be far greater than the value of the restored instrument. Consult an expert if you are in doubt. Major repairs and restoration should be done only by knowledgeable experts.

Before repairing a rare or valuable traverso, photographs should be taken of the instrument in its unrestored condition. Measurements of the inside and outside of the individual sections should also be made and recorded, preferably by an instrument-maker. If the instrument were ever to be copied, acquired by a museum, or studied by a scholar, these photographs and measurements would be a valuable part of its documentation.

Following is a check-list of matters to be considered for repair or improvement upon acquiring an antique.

1. The end cork stopper in the head piece should be properly fitted and made movable. Frequently the stopper in old flutes is immovable. If a light tap on a dowel placed against the cork cannot loosen it, then an expert may be needed to correct this condition. If the cork has dried out, it may have shrunk to the point of being too loose. An expert can correct this by replacing it with a new, properly cut cork.

2. Existing penetrating cracks need prompt attention. They occur most often from the stress set up when the inner layers of wood absorb moisture while the outer layers remain dry. Fine, non-penetrating cracks can usually be ignored, but in such cases, extra care should be taken to control temperature and humidity. Cracks can be repaired in many instances, but this should be left to an expert. In an emergency, keep the crack clean and cover it with electrician's plastic insulating tape or wind the piece with a non-adhesive plumber's plastic tape until an expert can repair it properly. There is a reasonable chance of successfully repairing a clean crack with one of the modern 'miracle' glues; however, it is usually difficult to keep the crack sealed using only glue. Many old flutes have cracks which have been repaired by pinning. Pinning is unsightly; furthermore, when the pin corrodes, it may break and complicate the problem. However, some technicians now use fine nylon pins to avoid the problem of corrosion. If a crack in the wood has advanced into the adjoining ivory socket ring, the ivory ring should be replaced completely; the original ring should be labelled and saved.

3. Key springs should operate efficiently, and pads on the keys should cover the tone holes without allowing any leakage. All key repair work should be done by the experts.

4. Socket rings and the end cap should be securely fitted. Silver or brass keys, silver socket rings and end cap (if any) may be cleaned and polished, provided cleaners are used which are intended for antiques. Frequently the end cap will be missing from an antique. Any good traverso-maker can fashion a replacement.

5. Replace old thread wrappings on tenons with new, using silk, linen, or cotton impregnated with beeswax. When all the old thread has been removed, clean the tenon of accumulated dirt and grease. The new wrapping will look more elegant if wound by an expert using a lathe, but doing it carefully by hand is also feasible. Friedrich von Huene suggests first applying a thin layer of solvent-based glue to hold down the initial layer of thread so that the tenon won't become jammed from freely turning wrappings. The thread should be

neat enough to ensure a smooth fit with the socket. Lightly lubricate the threads with cork grease or white petrolatum (petroleum jelly), preferably each time the instrument is assembled. Tenons should not be forced into sockets. The number of layers of thread on the tenon should ensure a good fit.

6. Improve the tuning of the instrument, if needed. Most antique flutes have a faulty scale, the result of countless years of normal use causing the interior dimensions to shrink slightly.[1] All shrinkage affects the tuning; as shrinkage is always uneven throughout the length of the tube, the scale is unevenly affected by it. To determine which note or notes are aberrant, carefully play the scale without 'favouring' any of the notes.

As a first corrective step, try alternative fingerings. If this is not practical or effective, then proceed as follows: cover a small part of the next available open hole on the instrument as a test of lowering the pitch of a note. For example, if a′ is too high, try covering a small part of the third hole. If this improves the relative pitch of a′ while not creating other intonation problems, then the diameter of this tone hole may be reduced slightly by using beeswax. To accomplish the tuning, melt beeswax over a flame and, using a sliver of wood such as bamboo or a toothpick, deposit the melted wax on the sides of the wall of the tone hole. Repeat the application as much as needed to reduce the diameter of the hole enough to lower the pitch of the note to the degree desired. Of course, when adjusting the size (or amount of undercutting) of a tone hole, one must also pay attention to the other notes on which that hole has an effect. Tuning an antique traverso is something that you can do for yourself, and it is perhaps best to do it over a period of days as you play the instrument under varying circumstances and become better acquainted with it. Tuning almost always involves pitch compromises. Never attempt to cut into the walls of the tone holes or embouchure of an antique in order to tune the instrument. In the past, many otherwise fine antique instruments were damaged, indeed, virtually destroyed, by well-meaning players who attempted to enlarge tone holes or the embouchure. If an antique cannot be tuned to your satisfaction by placing the cork stopper in the correct position and by altering the size of tone holes with wax, then you should consider acquiring a different instrument, antique or modern.

---

[1] Ardal Powell has written, 'The areas of the flute most drastically affected by shrinkage are those where antinodes in the air column most frequently occur in the bore (because they get wet first). The one part of the flute in which every note of the scale produces an antinode is a section two inches or so either side of the head-joint socket. Since this area is nearly always the first to be affected by shrinkage (noticeably at first when the octaves of a′ and b′ become too small, and a‴ gets higher) a useful trick is to play with the head-joint pulled out a fraction, effectively enlarging the bore at that point, and counteracting the slight general rise in pitch which the shrinkage brings about.' (Letter to author, 31 Aug. 1988.)

In principle, re-tuning a traverso by changing the undercutting or tone hole size is less effective than making small adjustments to the bore. However, while it is sometimes possible for an experienced flute-maker to salvage a faulty instrument by altering the bore, this is not to be encouraged on a do-it-yourself basis. In any case, the bores of antiques should not be re-reamed.

When a New Traverso Is Acquired

Acquiring a new traverso should involve no initial repairs. Coming directly from the maker or a dealer appointed by the maker, the instrument should be in perfect condition.

One of the first things to be examined is the placement of the cork stopper. Do not assume that its placement is right for you. The octaves d', d", and d''' should be in tune with each other when *you* play them. If not, then the location of the cork should be shifted to make them play in tune. To lower the pitch of d''', push the cork away from the embouchure hole towards the end cap. To raise d''', push the cork closer towards the embouchure hole. If your traverso does not have a screw cork, it is necessary to use a dowel (a wooden rod about 1.5 cm. (5/8") in diameter) to move the cork.

In the eighteenth century, makers and players apparently did conceive of a proper theoretical placement for the cork; the numbered, graduated cork stopper is evidence of that. However, experience has shown that there is no exact scientific location for the cork because of the human factor in playing: each player has a different tone-production technique which affects the cork's placement. Some play with tight, 'smiling' embouchures while others have relaxed, forward embouchures. Some players may force the low register in the manner of playing on the modern Boehm-system metal flute, thus causing it to become high in pitch relative to the other registers. Others may overblow the high register with similar results. Let your ear be the judge of your cork placement.[2]

One ought not take for granted the tuning of the new instrument which you are acquiring from a maker. Tuning involves aesthetic judgements, and there is no universal agreement about such matters. If you dislike the tuning of your instrument, discuss with the maker the possibility of changing it. (In any case, do not hesitate to send the instrument to the maker for a check-up and possible

---

[2] If you are acquiring a flute with a *corps de rechange* for playing at more than one pitch, placing a different upper middle piece in the traverso requires a change in the position of the cork in the head piece, as explained in Ch. 3. If your instrument also has a foot register, this, too, should be adjusted when changing the upper middle pieces.

re-reaming, if necessary, before the end of the first year of use.) By using beeswax, you yourself can reduce the size of specific tone holes and thereby change the tuning, as has been discussed in this chapter with regard to antique flutes.

Long-Term Maintenance

Once the traverso has been put into the best possible playing condition for you, there are certain procedures which will help to ensure that the instrument will not deteriorate with use.

1. Any wooden or ivory flute with an unsealed bore needs to be 'played in' gradually: ten minutes per session (maximum of two per day) for the first two weeks, then one thirty-minute session per day for another two weeks. One may possibly play it in faster without cracking it, but one must also consider the important element of minimizing the distortion of the bore. No wooden instrument should ever be played more than two hours per day, preferably no more than one. Just because an antique instrument has survived without cracking for centuries does not guarantee it against further cracking. If your traverso is not regularly played and has been allowed to dry out, play it in gradually again.

2. Always warm the instrument before playing. A cold instrument will condense your warm breath faster than a warm one. A cold instrument being warmed by playing will also be unstable in pitch while warming. Warm the instrument slowly by holding it in your hands or under your arm. Electrical heating rolls are a recent development which are designed to warm flutes or recorders prior to using them.

3. Keep the threads on the tenons adjusted so that the tenons will fit properly into the sockets. Unlike metal flutes, instruments of wood and ivory will shrink or expand with use and with changes in temperature and humidity. One should always have on hand a spool of thread to cope with these changes. Keep the thread wrappings well lubricated with cork grease or petroleum jelly.

4. Use a twisting motion to assemble or disassemble the traverso. Always disassemble the traverso immediately after playing. Failure to do so may result in the tenon becoming stuck in the socket. To free such a tenon, dry the inside of the instrument, then allow it to dry additionally at room temperature for several days before attempting to disassemble it.

5. The exterior and interior of the instrument should be oiled. Whenever the exterior appears dry or the finish becomes dull, apply a light coat of three parts boiled linseed oil thinned with one part turpentine. Oils applied to the

interior of a traverso act as a partial barrier to help prevent moisture from penetrating the wood. The application of oil to the bore of a traverso thus helps to prevent cracking. Note that it does not prevent it, it merely helps to prevent it. If the bore of a flute is permanently sealed with a varnish, it does not require oiling. Experts are in disagreement about what kind of oil to apply to the inside of a bore if the instrument is not permanently sealed. Some prefer a mixture of linseed oil and turpentine. Linseed oil is a drying oil, first becoming sticky and then hard like a varnish. This gives a somewhat brighter sound to the traverso, since the degree of porosity of the interior of the bore affects the tone. Other experts state that linseed oil, by eventually drying in the wood, may crack it. They recommend instead almond, peanut, or olive oil. (Quantz recommended almond oil; Tromlitz stated that almond oil is too thin and dries too fast. What one needs ideally is a slightly acidic non-drying oil.) When oiling a bore, first make sure that the wood is dry and hasn't been played for a few hours. Let the oil remain in the bore for at least two hours—overnight is better—then remove the excess. The bore of a new instrument should be oiled weekly or monthly until it will not absorb any more. Check for dry patches where the oil has been fully absorbed and more should be added.

6. Avoid extremes of temperature and humidity, or sudden changes. Because wood and ivory react noticeably to such things, it is common sense to minimize variations in humidity and temperature. If you live in a climate with hot, humid summers and cold, dry winters, it is especially advisable to stabilize the humidity and temperature as much as possible. Steam heating is particularly stressful on wooden or ivory instruments unless the air is humidified. Ideal conditions are 68°F (20°C) and 50 per cent relative humidity. Above all, avoid placing the instrument on or near direct sources of heat, such as radiators or vents. When not in use (especially in winter), a traverso should be kept in an airtight plastic bag to help stabilize the moisture content, if you are in a geographic location of relatively low humidity. In a damp climate, a cloth or sheepskin roll-up bag provides the best protection, allowing moisture to flow to and fro.

7. Avoid drafts. The moving air originating from an open window, electric fan, or air-conditioner will quickly dry out an instrument and increase the risk of cracking.

8. Avoid direct sunlight. A traverso carelessly placed so that the direct rays of the sun hit it runs the risk of cracking.

9. Remove moisture from the instrument immediately upon cessation of playing. Even if only setting the instrument aside for a few brief minutes, one should swab out the inside of the instrument. As stated before, cracking is most often caused by humidity-induced stresses in the wood or ivory which occur when the inside of the bore is wet and the outside is dry. The best swab to use

is a piece of silk, cotton, or linen cloth threaded through the eye of a swab stick. Avoid denting the cork when swabbing. Do not use woollen swabs, as wool does not absorb moisture. Swabbing also helps to remove dirt or grime which may have accumulated inside the instrument. Always inspect the inside of the instrument to make sure that it has been thoroughly dried.

10. Do not let lipstick or ink come into contact with your traverso. Ivory and wood are very absorbent. A permanent stain will result if an instrument is used by a player wearing lipstick. Ink from a fountain pen or ball-point pen will also leave permanent marks on an ivory instrument.

11. Always carry your traverso in a proper case or bag. The most popular carrying cases today are the waterproof tote bags with sheepskin lining with individual compartments for each of the instrument's pieces. Jean Cavallaro of 20 Vernon Street, Somerville, MA 02145, USA, makes these instrument rolls. They are made of waterproof nylon duck and are available in a variety of sizes.

12. Avoid subjecting your traverso to excessive travel resulting in changes in humidity and temperature. Antiques are especially vulnerable in this regard. If you have both antique and modern instruments, leave the antiques at home and travel with your replicas.

13. If a crack appears in your instrument, do not attempt to repair it yourself. Only an expert should do such a repair. Be sure to keep the crack clean.

14. If the pitch of a new instrument rises permanently—for example, if an A=415 traverso eventually plays at A=420 on a regular basis—then it either means that the maker did not use properly dry, seasoned wood, or that the buyer played it in too quickly. In this case, you should return the instrument to the maker to have the bore re-reamed. Do not re-ream antique instruments.

15. On rare occasions a key may stick or the spring may break or become too weak to keep the key closed. The remedy, in an emergency, is to wrap a rubber band around the instrument, encompassing the flap of the key. This will close the key as if the spring were working. If the loss of tension is caused by a weakening of the spring, it is possible to remove the key and bend the spring, gently and smoothly, to renew its thrust.

7
Sources: Technique

THE technique of playing baroque and classical flutes is well served by primary sources dating from the period under consideration in this book. Although few of these sources were originally written in English, many have now been translated. Of the original source materials in English included in this chapter, only those available in modern reprint are discussed. A few treatises exist only in the original language (usually French). Some of these will be commented upon here because they are available in facsimile editions and contain easily understood fingering charts as well as musical examples which are useful as learning material.

Secondary sources for traverso technique remain sparce. To date, only two secondary source books have appeared: *The Baroque Flute Fingering Book* by Margaret Neuhaus, published in 1986, and *A Practical & Tuneful Method for the Baroque Flute* by Peter H. Bloom, published in 1989. In addition to its great value as a secondary source for fingerings, Neuhaus's book illustrates an important truth about the search for answers from primary sources concerning traverso techniques (and style), i.e. the broad diversity of opinions which these original sources offer us, reflecting the individuality which existed among performers in the centuries previous to ours.

Caution should always be exercised in the practical application of information from original sources. The facts and ideas presented should be viewed from a wider historical perspective. What may be true for one time, place, or instrument may or may not be true for another time, place, or instrument. For example, the range of standard fingering options available for the baroque and classical flute is much greater than for the modern Boehm-system flute. Seemingly identical instruments may sometimes respond differently to the same fingering. The same instrument with different centre pieces (thereby playing at different pitches) may require different fingerings for the same note or trill. Moreover, differences of style are even more subtle and complicated than technique. (See Chapter 8.)[1]

---

[1] Although articulation is both a technique and a style, for the purposes of this book it will be considered in Ch. 8, which discusses style.

Primary Sources in English Translation

The earliest known source for baroque flute technique is found not in a tutor but in the preface to Michel de la Barre's 1702 *Pieces pour la flute traversiere, avec la basse-continue*, the first publication to appear specifically indicating the one-keyed transverse flute as a solo instrument. The preface is published in English translation in the edition of de la Barre's *Pieces* prepared by Jane Bowers for Heugel (Paris, 1978). De la Barre's preface includes only one specific piece of advice concerning technique, namely, how to play c#′ on an instrument the lowest natural note of which is d′. (The answer is to roll the embouchure of the flute inward.) In a note of disarming sincerity, de la Barre explains that he does not know how to explain in writing the fingerings for e‴ and d#‴. He therefore suggests that the reader should call at his house so that he may demonstrate how it is done, without charge.[2]

● Jacques Hotteterre le Romain, *Principles of the Flute, Recorder & Oboe*, trans. and ed. David Lasocki (London: Barrie & Rockliff/The Cresset Press, 1968)

● Jacques-Martin Hotteterre, *Rudiments of the Flute, Recorder & Oboe*, trans., with introduction and notes, by Paul Marshall Douglas (New York: Dover Publications, 1968; repr. 1983 as *Principles of the Flute, Recorder & Oboe*)

Hotteterre, who was de la Barre's colleague at the court of Louis XIV, wrote the first treatise concerning the technique and style of traverso-playing. He discusses such technical matters as hand position, posture, tone production, and embouchure. He includes a fingering chart for all of the notes of the chromatic scale from d′ to g‴ with the exception of f‴, which he omits from the chart because of its difficulty on the flute of his time. He describes the fingering in the text, however. He also discusses ways of improving the intonation of certain notes and trills by rolling the flute inward or outward. One should note the enharmonic fingerings: f#′ and f#″ are fingered differently from g♭′ and g♭″; c#‴ is fingered differently from d♭‴. Also included are a chart and a verbal explanation for all of the trills from d′ to f#‴.[3]

---

[2] Charles Nicholson, in his *Preceptive Lessons for the Flute* (1821), makes a similar offer in writing (p. 26): 'Convinced however, how very inferior all written precepts are to oral instruction . . . and willing as far as possible to be serviceable to those Amateurs who may follow the course of Practice pointed out in these Preceptive Lessons, he [the author] will have much pleasure in giving a Lesson gratis on the formation of the Embouchure etc., to all who may possess the Work when complete; and by One Lesson on this subject he feels assured that a Pupil will derive more benefit than if he were at the trouble to peruse a whole Volume.'

[3] A useful chart for ornaments appears in the 1715 second edition of Hotteterre's *Premier livre de pieces pour la Flûte-traversiere*, reprinted in facsimile by Studio per Edizione Scelte (Florence, 1980). The chart is also printed in the introduction to the Heugel edition of de la Barre's *Pieces pour la flute traversiere* and in the preface to Bärenreiter's edition of Hotteterre's Suite in E minor.

The remainder of the text concerns matters of style, as well as brief treatises on the recorder and the oboe. The technique explained in Hotteterre's treatise pertains to the three-piece Hotteterre-type flute pitched at around A=392 to A=405 which was in use at the French court for about fifty years (*c.*1670–1720). (See Figs. 6–9.) These fingerings for notes and trills may or may not be valid for non-French flutes made during this time or for any flutes made after about 1720. The geometry of the instrument differed from country to country and changed with the years as tastes changed, especially with regard to tuning and temperament. Therefore, one must not assume that Hotteterre's fingerings are correct for any traverso other than Hotteterre-type French flutes.

● Michel Corrette, *Method for Easily Learning to Play on the Transverse Flute*, trans. Carol Reglin Farrar (Brooklyn, NY: Institute of Medieval Music, 1970).
Corrette (1709–95) was a French organist and composer who wrote methods for a number of instruments, including flute, oboe, violin, violoncello, harpsichord, and vielle. His *Methode* for flute was published in Paris *c.*1740 and represents a somewhat later approach to the traverso than Hotteterre's treatise presented. The instrument considered here is the four-piece one-keyed traverso. (This confirms that by the late 1730s the three-piece flute of Hotteterre's era had been replaced in France by a standardized four-piece instrument.)

The technical aspects of flute-playing covered in this treatise include holding the flute, acquiring an embouchure, and charts for the fingerings of chromatic scales and trills, as well as explanations of fingerings for *flattements* and *battements*. Corrette's fingerings do not always agree with those of Hotteterre twenty-eight years earlier; the 'modernized' design of the traverso would have been partly responsible for this. Another contributing factor to this difference is that Corrette seeks an 'easy' method, simplifying syllables for articulation and eliminating the several enharmonic fingerings which had been noted by Hotteterre. Although acknowledging the existence of such distinctions in the scale of his time, Corrette does not think that the traverso player should be concerned about them.

Ms Farrar's translation is frequently inaccurate and misleading. For those who cannot read Corrette's treatise in the original French, it may be advisable to avoid her English translation because of its many mistakes and shortcomings. Her introductory remarks regarding the flauto traverso are insensitive if not callous: 'an instrument with more imperfections than merits ... that rather hindered good playing than promoted it'.[4]

---

[4] Introduction to Corrette, *Method for Easily Learning to Play on the Transverse Flute*, trans. Carol Reglin Farrar (Brooklyn: Institute of Medieval Music, 1970), 13.

●Johann Joachim Quantz, *On Playing the Flute*, trans. with notes and an introduction by Edward R. Reilly (London: Faber & Faber, 1966, 1985; New York: Free Press, 1966, Schirmer Books, 1985).

After the brevity of the Hotteterre and Corrette treatises—both are less than fifty pages long in their original editions—the extraordinary breadth of Quantz's (1697–1773) treatise (comprising 334 pages of text, a 20-page index, and 24 plates of charts and music) is impressive. Quantz's celebrated essay is not merely a tutor for the traverso player; it addresses itself to a broader readership including musicians of all persuasions. The noted Quantz authority, Edward R. Reilly, has observed that of the eighteen chapters in the book, only a handful deal exclusively with flute matters. The rest cover such topics as note values and musical signs, articulation, appoggiaturas and other short graces, how to play an allegro and an adagio, cadenzas, free ornamentation, accompanying, musical forms and styles, and general advice to anyone who wants to become a musician.

Chapters which consider the technique of traverso-playing give practical advice for holding the flute, the placement of the fingers, fingerings for scales and trills (but not *flattements*), and the embouchure. These technical instructions represent an extraordinary refinement of the art of flute-playing. What distinguishes Quantz's treatise (in addition to its sheer breadth and scope) are the technical demands that it places on players who attempt to incorporate Quantz's highly refined teaching into their playing. Corrette seeks the 'easy' way to play the flute whereas Quantz teaches the artful way. His technical advice reflects his life's experience as flautist, teacher, and composer. As a young man, he travelled extensively in Italy, France, and England, meeting many of the greatest living musicians. As a member of the Dresden orchestra, he worked with and studied under Buffardin, the well-known French flute virtuoso who brought to Saxony the traditions which had already begun to be established at the French court. As a mature professional, he worked as court musician at one of Europe's most important centres. The flute which Quantz designed and made fulfilled his needs as a performer; however, the instrument was not typical of mid-eighteenth-century flutes. Recent measurements of an existing Quantz flute[5] reveal that the diameter of the bore at the head piece is greater than in other flutes made at the same time, and the degree of tapering to the foot piece is also greater. Quantz also preferred the lower pitches associated with the French court (A=392–A=415). His concept of flute sound was a product of his French orientation. He insisted too upon distinguishing between enharmonic sharps

[5] Michael Seyfrit, *Musical Instruments in the Dayton C. Miller Collection at the Library of Congress*, i (Washington, DC, Library of Congress, 1982), pp. xviii–xix.

and flats. All of these facts had an effect upon the sound, scale, and tessitura of Quantz's flute. Necessarily, his fingering charts reflect this fastidious taste.

- Antoine Mahaut, *A New Method for Learning to Play the Transverse Flute*, trans. and ed. Eileen Hadidian (Bloomington, Ind.: Indiana University Press, 1989).
In his introduction, Mahaut praises Hotteterre's treatise but says that since the flute has been brought to a high standard and the Italian musical style has become so influential, the Hotteterre treatise is out of date. The text, originally published in 1759, is augmented with fingering charts for the chromatic scale from c♯' to d'''' and for trills. The latter includes 134 different trill fingerings, with as many as six alternative fingerings for one trilled interval. Mahaut includes enharmonic fingerings for eight notes to differentiate between the sharp and its enharmonic flat. Following the technical and stylistic chapters, there are thirty-five pages of music, consisting of flute duets.

- Johann George Tromlitz, *The Virtuoso Flute-Player*, trans. and ed. Ardal Powell, introduction by Eileen Hadidian (Cambridge: Cambridge University Press, 1991).[6]
This treatise, which appeared in 1791 under the title *Ausführlicher und gründlicher Unterricht die Flöte zu spielen*, is the second most important flute tutor of the eighteenth century. Tromlitz was a Leipzig flautist, teacher, writer, and maker of flutes. In the latter capacity, he contributed to the development of the transverse flute, including the invention of the long F key. Whereas Quantz's treatise was written on the premiss that it is a supplement to studying with a teacher, Tromlitz wrote his extensive tutor complete unto itself with no teacher required. (Tromlitz said, however, that the student should choose the best teacher if at all possible.) Tromlitz emulates Quantz, taking from Quantz's treatise whatever he regards as usable and indicating that which he thinks should be changed. Like Quantz, he recommends the use of a flute with two keys on the foot piece to differentiate between e♭ and d♯.

Tromlitz's chapters on technique include discussions of tone production, embouchure, and fingering. His fingerings are for the two-keyed Quantz-type flute, although in earlier and later publications he discusses in great detail flutes with four or more keys.[7] He also points out that because each flute is tuned somewhat differently from any other, one single set of fingerings for all flutes would not be feasible.

---

[6] Another translation of this book was made by Linda Bishop Hartig in partial fulfilment of requirements for a doctorate in 1981. It is available from University Microfilms, Ann Arbor, Mich.

[7] The other books by Tromlitz are *Kurze Abhandlung vom Flötenspielen* (1786), which announces the invention of the long F key, and *Ueber die Flöten mit mehrern Klappen* (1800).

English Tutors

Many flute tutors appeared in England during the eighteenth century, obviously in an attempt to satisfy the demands of great numbers of amateur traverso players. Most of these tutors were written anonymously and bear such titles as the 'Compleat Tutor for the German Flute' or 'New Instructions for the German Flute'. Some of the English tutors with known authors have been made available in recent years in facsimile editions, among which are the following.

- Peter Prelleur, *The Newest Method for Learners on the German Flute*, from *The Modern Musick-Master or The Universal Musician* (1731); facsimile edn. (Kassel: Bärenreiter, 1965).

- Luke Heron, *A Treatise on the German Flute* (1771); facsimile edn. (Buren: Frits Knuf, 1973).

- John Gunn, *The Art of Playing the German Flute* (*c.*1793); facsimile edn. (Marion, Ia.: Janice Dockendorff Boland).

Prelleur's treatise borrows heavily from Hotteterre's *Principes*, which had been printed in English in 1729; in fact, it has even been called a pirated edition.[8] However, Prelleur does not always agree with Hotteterre regarding fingerings. Much more original is Luke Heron's treatise, which includes material on the ancient modes and on accompanying, as well as the usual matters of fingerings, ornaments, articulation, rhythm, and scales. Gunn's tutor, which gives fingerings for flutes with from one to six keys, contains some material virtually copied (with acknowledgement) from Quantz's treatise, especially the chapter on free ornamentation or embellishment. However, there is much material in Gunn's book which represents new thought regarding the technique of flute-playing. Especially with regard to sound and tone production, Gunn explains concepts which are a marked development over Quantz's ideas. Gunn differentiates between velocity of breath and quantity of air and relates these to the diameter of the air column (determined by the aperture of the lips) and the direction of the column, all of which have an effect upon sound. He writes of the 'intensity of sound, which depends solely on the *density* or compression of the air' and he distinguishes between loudness produced by a more dense air column and loudness produced by an increase in the volume of air. He notes that these 'produce very different effects on the ear.' These observations are original for

[8] Dayton C. Miller, *Catalogue of Books and Literary Material Relating to the Flute and Other Musical Instruments* (Cleveland, Oh.: privately printed, 1935), 79. Miller refers to Prelleur's book as 'clearly a pirated edition, with the omission of the author's portrait, of the English edition of Hotteterre'.

the most part[9] and are concepts which have been fundamental to the teaching of influential twentieth-century flautists such as William Kincaid.[10]

There are other treatises in English which include commentary about the technique of one- to eight-keyed flutes. Among these are Lewis Granom's *Plain and Easy Instructions for Playing on the German-Flute* (1766); J. Wragg's *The Flute Preceptor*, a popular tutor which appeared in no less than thirteen editions between 1792 and 1795 and thrice that number by the second half of the nineteenth century; Tebaldo Monzani's *Instructions for the German Flute* (1801); John Beale's *A Complete Guide to the Art of Playing the German Flute* (*c*.1815); Charles Nicholson's *Complete Preceptor for the German Flute* (*c*.1816, with later editions); R. W. Keith's *A New and Complete Preceptor for the German Flute* (1816–22); and James Alexander's *Alexander's Complete Preceptor for the Flute* (1821). These treatises are not yet available in modern reprint and are thus not within the scope of this book. It is to be hoped that some if not all of these tutors will be reprinted in facsimile in the next few years.

Primary Sources in French

Following are selected primary sources in French which have been reprinted in facsimile editions. The fingering charts and music in these treatises are useful to all students of the traverso, even those who do not read French.

• De Lusse, *L'Art de la flûte traversiere* (Paris, *c*.1760); facsimile edns. (Columbus, Oh.: Early Music Facsimiles; Buren: Frits Knuf, 1980; Geneva: Minkoff, 1973).

De Lusse (whose first name, according to Fetis, was Charles) became flautist of the Opéra Comique in Paris around 1758. About 1760 he published his *L'Art de la flûte traversiere*, which contains fingering charts for the chromatic scale from d′ to a♯‴ and fifty-nine different trill fingerings. The musical portion of the book includes twenty-eight 'lessons' of music (consisting mostly of duets for flute and bass), twenty preludes, each in a different key, and twelve

---

[9] It should be noted that an article by F. D. Castilon appeared in the third volume of the *Supplément to Diderot's Encyclopédie*. The text, translated by Eric Halfpenny for his article 'A French Commentary on Quantz' in *Music & Letters*, 37 (1956), includes the following: 'Three things contribute to tone-production on the flute: the volume of wind, its velocity and the way the lips form and control the embouchure. To produce the octave of a note on a wind instrument, one must cause the column of air to vibrate at twice its former speed, and this depends on the velocity of the wind. This was shown by Vaucanson's famous flute-playing automaton, where he caused twice as much wind to pass in the same time in the same tube to obtain the octave. The wind, passing the same opening, therefore acquired twice the velocity. If the same volume of wind is doubled in velocity it produces the same effect; and to do this it is only necessary to reduce the size of the orifice through which the wind escapes, and that is exactly what a good flute player does.'

[10] See John Krell, *Kincaidiana* (Culver City, Calif.: Trio Associates, 1973), 9–10.

caprices designed as exercises for embouchure and fingers. De Lusse suggests they may also be used as cadenzas for flute concertos. Appended to the treatise is a unique piece of music from the eighteenth century, a quarter-tone piece called *Air à la Grecque* for flute and bass. A table of fingerings for the transverse flute is included which gives the fingerings for all the notes in the diatonic, chromatic, and enharmonic genera. The enharmonic fingerings produce the quarter-tone intervals which are the fascinating feature of this short work.

- F. Devienne, *Nouvelle Méthode Théorique et Pratique Pour La Flute* (Paris: Imbault, *c*.1794); facsimile edns. (Florence: Studio per Edizioni Scelte, 1984; Buren, Frits Knuf, forthcoming).

- J. M. Cambini, *Methode pour la Flûte traversiere* (Paris: Gaveaux, *c*.1796–7); facsimile edn. (Florence; Studio per Edizione Scelte, 1984).

- Amand Vanderhagen, *Nouvelle Méthode de Flute* (Paris: Pleyel, *c*.1799); facsimile edn. (Florence: Studio per Edizione Scelte, 1984).

These three treatises were published in Paris in the last decade of the eighteenth century and have been issued in a facsimile edition (as a set) by Marcello Castellani for Studio per Edizioni Scelte as *Tre Metodi per Flauto del Neoclassicismo Francese* (1984). The fingering charts for all of these methods are for the one-keyed traverso, an indication that the Parisian flautists preferred to play one-keyed instruments to the very end of the eighteenth century. The multi-keyed flutes which had been in vogue in England since the 1770s had not yet made an impact in France.

Devienne (1759–1803) was a leading Parisian flautist and bassoonist, in addition to being a prolific composer of operas and instrumental music. His flute method (in its original version as well as adapted for the Boehm-system flute by subsequent generations) has remained in print virtually continuously until the present day—a run of nearly two centuries! Included in the original method are fingering charts for the chromatic scale and for trills. The duets for two flutes include twenty *petits airs*, eighteen duos of a more advanced nature, and six sonatas for two flutes.

Cambini (1746–1825) was a violinist and composer, not a flautist. Perhaps for this reason his tutor for flute has little to offer the player concerning technique other than a table of fingerings for the chromatic scale. No trill fingerings are included. The volume concludes with twenty *petits airs* and six duos for two flutes.

Vanderhagen (1753–1822), a celebrated Belgian-born clarinettist, worked in Paris and is credited with having published the first tutor for the clarinet (1785). The *Nouvelle Méthode* for flute includes a fingering chart for the chromatic scale from d′ to bb‴ and a table for trill fingerings. Vanderhagen's material is very similar to Devienne's method and reveals his familiarity with Devienne's book. About one-third of the book consists of short pieces arranged as duets for two flutes—the favourite pedagogical device of French flautists at this time.

- A. Hugot and J. C. Wunderlich, *Méthode de Flûte* (Paris, 1804); facsimile edn., with an introduction by David Jenkins (Buren: Frits Knuf, 1975).
Hugot and Wunderlich were professors of flute at the Paris Conservatoire at the end of the eighteenth century and the first part of the nineteenth. Hugot commenced the writing of this tutor. After his untimely death in 1803, Wunderlich completed it. In 1804 it was accepted by the Paris Conservatoire as its official flute instruction book. The treatise is important because, rather than being a reworking of earlier methods, it is a completely fresh work which serves to introduce the four-keyed flute. It is the finest tutor for the four-keyed instrument and contains tables of fingerings for both the one- and four-keyed flutes, in addition to over a hundred pages of pieces skilfully designed to develop the student's facility. Hugot and Wunderlich prefer the four-keyed flute to the six-keyed flute with the foot extension to low c′; the extended foot piece upsets the diapason of the instrument.

In his informative introduction in English, David Jenkins points out how this treatise illustrates the development of the transverse flute in the ninety-seven years since the appearance of Hotteterre's treatise. Whereas the contemporary reader of Hotteterre's book was primarily the amateur flautist, Hugot and Wunderlich wrote for the aspiring professional. By this time there was a professional need for conservatory-trained flautists. The flute had now become an established part of the orchestra.

Jenkins also observes that the Hugot–Wunderlich tutor does not contain the careful attention to such stylistic matters as unwritten rhythmic conventions, ornamentation, and patterns of articulation which play such a prominent part in the treatises of Hotteterre, Quantz, and C. P. E. Bach. Performing practices had become more carefully notated by 1800, with less need for explanations of conventions of performance. This greater simplicity is evident in the content of the Hugot–Wunderlich tutor, which places more emphasis on the development of technical facility on the four-keyed flute.

Secondary Sources in English

- Margaret N. Neuhaus, *The Baroque Flute Fingering Book* (Naperville, Ill.: Flute Studio Press, 1986). This is an important, indeed indispensable secondary source in English for the technique of the transverse flute.[11] Although the title

[11] For a book review by John Solum, see the *Newsletter* of the American Musical Instrument Society, 16: 2 (June 1987), 13.

implies that the book is limited to the baroque flute, it includes fingerings for the classical one-keyed flute as well. The subtitle more accurately defines the scope of the book: 'A comprehensive guide to fingerings for the one-keyed flute including trills, flattements, and battements based on original sources from the eighteenth and nineteenth centuries'.

Ms Neuhaus has collated fingerings for the one-keyed flute from twenty-one original sources dating from 1707 to *c*.1825, including the flute tutors of Hotteterre, Corrette, Quantz, Mahaut, De Lusse, Tromlitz, Gunn, Devienne, Hugot–Wunderlich, and Nicholson, among others. Since many of the treatises offer more than one fingering for some notes or ornaments, and since there is much difference of opinion between the treatises regarding fingerings, frequently a large number of fingerings must be given for any specific note or ornament. For example, there are thirteen different fingerings for c''' and eleven different fingerings for the b''/c♯''' trill. Each fingering chart always indicates in chronological order the sources of each fingering. Therefore, it is possible to see how tastes in fingerings or ornaments changed during the era of the one-keyed flute, and also how the physical changes in the one-keyed flute over a period of more than a century affected the fingerings.

The book includes descriptive statements regarding each of the sources as well as a reproduction of the title-page of each. The one unpublished source which Ms Neuhaus draws upon is a fingering chart by Quantz which was used by Frederick the Great; it was signed and dated by the King on 17 January 1753. It is now in the Staatlichen Instituts für Musikforschung-Preussischer Kulturbesitz, Berlin. The final part of the book gives special fingerings to facilitate the playing of difficult passages. These fingerings are found in the treatises of Quantz, Mahaut, Devienne, and Alexander.

• Peter H. Bloom, *A Practical & Tuneful Method for the Baroque Flute* (Somerville, Mass.: Peter H. Bloom, 1989).

This is the first modern tutor for the baroque flute, written by an accomplished player and experienced teacher. It is an elementary method designed for the beginner who has no previous experience in playing *any* flute but is able to read music. The topics covered (with the aid of illustrative photographs and drawings) include tone production, holding the flute, articulation, and how to practice. The musical part of the book is selected from eighteenth- and nineteenth-century sources and includes easy solos and duets.

Conclusion

Considering the great diversity of advice for the technique of traverso playing, one must learn to make personal choices. For all the rules that the treatises give, one must remember that flute-playing is an art, not a science. For those who seek authenticity, subjective choice is part of that authenticity. The writers of the original treatises give us the possibilities, but the modern performer must choose what is best for his or her instrument and what is most appropriate for the music to be performed. Major factors in determining these choices are the sounds that one hears and the taste that is acquired through practice and experience. As Quantz writes, 'Anyone who does not wish to trust my taste . . . is free to try the opposite of that which I teach, and then choose what seems best to him.[12]

[12] J. J. Quantz, *On Playing the Flute*, ed. and trans. Edward R. Reilly (London: Faber & Faber, 1966; 2nd edn., 1985), 8.

8

Sources: Style

ONE of the pleasures of playing baroque and classical music on period instruments is that it leads us again and again into considerations of style. Because we do not have recordings from the pre-Romantic era (except what is revealed to us by mechanical musical instruments such as barrel organs), we are therefore largely dependent upon contemporary written information to tell us how music was played or sung. (We can also determine certain things from the instruments themselves, from pictures and engravings, and especially from a careful study of the written music.) Since those who wrote about such matters in the baroque and classical ages frequently disagreed amongst themselves about what constituted correct style, and since modern scholars are certainly not in agreement about how to interpret those writings, it makes a very lively field of enquiry for any musician involved in historically informed performance.

Each country or region had its own set of performance practices, and the application of these 'rules' changed with each passing decade. What may have been good style for Michel de la Barre in Paris in 1702 may not have been acceptable to François Devienne in the same city a century later. Even two or more composer-performers working at the same place and the same time (such as C. P. E. Bach and Quantz at the court of Frederick the Great) did not agree on all aspects of style. Further complications arise when we observe that composers of one nationality wrote in the style of another, such as when a German, J. S. Bach, composed a French ouverture-suite for flauto traverso and strings or when a Frenchman, Michel Blavet, published flute sonatas (Op. 3) in the Italian style with Italian titles.

Among the many meanings of style found in the dictionary, the following definition is most pertinent to our consideration: 'A manner or method of acting or performing especially as recognized or sanctioned by some standard . . . one that is distinctive or characteristic of or attributed to some group or period.'[1] Style in musical performance involves such matters as ornamentation, rhythm, articulation, tempo, instrumentation, temperament, and harmonic realization.

---

[1] Webster's *Third International Dictionary* (Springfield, Mass.: G. & C. Merriam, 1968).

There are numerous primary and secondary sources in English for the study of baroque and classical performance style. It is possible to build a small home library of the most important of these for a relatively modest amount of money. More important than possessing them is a careful *reading* of them. To read all of the books discussed in this chapter is perhaps equivalent to a one-term course in a university. If one spends ten years or more mastering one's instrument, is it asking too much to spend a few hours per week for a few months to learn the fundamentals of style for performing baroque and classical music? It is useful to have read not only the original sources but also to be familiar with the viewpoints which have been presented by the performers and musicologists of the past hundred years who have attempted to interpret and organize the primary sources into a cohesive entity. Controversy abounds in this field (as indeed it did in the baroque and classical ages), and as a performer it is important to be aware of the options.

Primary Sources

Following is a selected list, in chronological order of publication, of important primary source materials published in English translation (if not originally written in English) which are applicable to baroque and classical flutes. Full bibliographic information is included only for sources not mentioned in Chapter 7. Some of these sources do not deal directly with the traverso. However, since the style which was cultivated by a singer or a player of one instrument was essentially applicable to all instruments of the same time and place, sources other than flute treatises are important to the study of style in traverso playing.

- Michel de la Barre, *Pieces pour la flute traversiere*.
  Michel de la Barre's short preface to his *Pieces pour la flute traversiere* (1702) contains the first stylistic advice specifically intended for the baroque flute, including the use of articulations (tonguing and slurring), when to trill, and instrumentation. De la Barre states that one may play most of these pieces without accompaniment. If there is accompaniment, it must include a bass viol, and a theorbo or a harpsichord, or both. The theorbo, however, is preferable because its gut strings sound better with the traverso than do the brass strings of the harpsichord.

- Jacques Hotteterre le Romain, *Principes de la flute traversiere*.
  Hotteterre's *Principes* (1707) is acknowledged to be the first tutor for the transverse flute. Although it is primarily concerned with technique, such stylistic matters as articulation and ornamentation are discussed and illustrated. Among the ornaments considered are the *port-de-voix* (appoggiatura), *double cadence*

(trill with termination), *coulement* (descending passing notes), *flattement* (finger vibrato), and *battement* (mordent). One should keep in mind that Hotteterre's advice pertains to the instruments and music of the age of Louis XIV in France. While some of this material may also be valid for the music of other countries and later periods, caution should be exercised in making blanket applications of Hotteterre's principles.[2]

- Pier Francesco Tosi, *Observations on the Florid Song*, trans. into English by J. C. Galliard (London: J. Wilcox, 1742; 2nd edn., 1743; repr. London: William Reeves, 1967; and London: Stainer & Bell, 1987). This book originally appeared in Italian (Bologna, 1723).
  Tosi (1646–1732) was an Italian singer and teacher who travelled widely and lived for many years in London. The preface states that the remarks contained in the book will be advantageous both to vocal and instrumental performers 'where Taste and a Manner are required'. Tosi writes about such stylistic matters as the appoggiatura, shakes (trills), divisions, recitative, cadenzas, graces, and airs (da capo arias). One shortcoming in Tosi's treatise is its lack of musical illustrations. An oft-quoted statement (ch. 11, sect. 41) concerns what we today call rubato: 'Whoever does not know how to steal the Time in Singing, knows not how to Compose, nor to Accompany himself, and is destitute of the best Taste and greatest Knowledge.'

- Michel Corrette, *Method for Easily Learning to Play on the Transverse Flute*.
  Corrette's method for flute (*c.*1740) considers such stylistic matters as *port-de-voix, accent, martellement, flattement, battement,* articulation, and preluding. He seems to promote a simplified approach to flute playing, as exemplified both in the title (*aisément*—'easily') and in the text. For example, he dismisses the 'former' way of articulation using two syllables (*tu* and *ru*), as recommended by Hotteterre. By implication, Corrette suggests that one syllable should suffice for all articulations.
  The chapter on preluding, which contains twenty-nine examples of preludes for the traverso, is further evidence of the popularity of playing a short warm-up exercise before beginning to play a piece. (Jean-Pierre Freillon-Poncein had published an oboe–recorder–flageolet tutor in 1700 including forty-one preludes, and Hotteterre's essay of 1719 is entirely devoted to preluding.) Corrette's

---

[2] Another valuable primary source for style is Hotteterre's *L'Art de Preluder sur la Flûte Traversiere, sur la Flûte a bec, sur le Haubois, et autres Instrumens de Dessus*, Op. 7 (1719), which has not yet been published in English translation. A facsimile of the original edition was published by Minkoff, Geneva, in 1978, and a slightly abridged modern edition was published by Michel Sanvoisin for Éditions Zurfluh in Paris in 1966. This work is important in explaining about the practice of improvisation of preludes; moreover, it discusses transposition, meter, and rhythmic inequality and provides a large number of practice studies.

chapter on rhythm points out some of the differences between Italian and French music and gives a few rules for the use of *notes inégales*.

- Francesco Geminiani, *The Art of Playing on the Violin* (1751); facsimile edn., ed. David D. Boyden (London: Oxford University Press, 1952).
  Although primarily a book of instructions for the technique of violin-playing, this short work has many valuable insights into music and musical performance. The opening sentence of Geminiani's preface is a statement which is good advice for any musician: 'The Intention of Musick is not only to please the Ear, but to express Sentiments, strike the Imagination, affect the Mind, and command the Passions.'

  Matters of style appear in a section on 'Ornaments of Expression', which includes shakes, appoggiaturas, staccato, swelling and softening, dynamics, and vibrato ('the close shake'), among others. The introduction by David Boyden is filled with interesting commentary and keen observation.

- Johann Joachim Quantz, *On Playing the Flute*.
  With the exception of a handful of relatively short chapters concerning the technique of playing the traverso, the major portion of Quantz's treatise (1752) concerns musical style. The book is one of the foremost sources for information about eighteenth-century style, representing the viewpoint of an important musician who worked in two major musical centres, Dresden and Berlin. However, Quantz had travelled widely and had met many of the most important composers and musicians of his day. His viewpoint in many respects represents both a broad and a detailed understanding of musical style of the mid-eighteenth century throughout Europe.

  The first ten chapters of the book are devoted to rudimentary musical matters; half of them are concerned with fundamental flute technique. The other half discuss stylistic matters, including rests and their value, metre and signs, articulation, taking a breath in the stylistic sense of where it should best be done, and appoggiaturas and the small fixed ornaments. Quantz includes detailed instructions for using syllables for musical articulation. 'The liveliness of the execution depends less upon the fingers than upon the tongue,' states Quantz (p. 71). These ten chapters also include useful illustrative musical examples and general information which is vital for informed baroque performance.

  The remaining eight chapters (comprising approximately two-thirds of the text) cover style as it applies to all instruments involved in musical performance, including the voice. Among the topics discussed are rules of good execution in singing and playing, how to play an allegro and an adagio, how to introduce extemporized embellishments on various intervals (see Fig. 34), and advice on

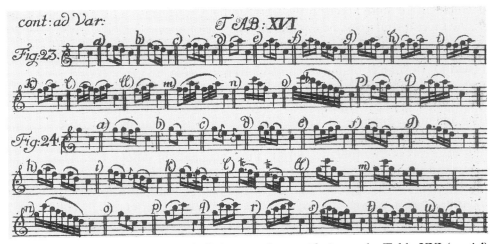

F IG . 34.   Two examples of embellishments for specific intervals, Table XVI (partial) from Johann Joachim Quantz, *Versuch einer Anweisung die Flöte traversiere zu spielen* (Berlin, 1752). Private collection

creating and playing cadenzas. The penultimate chapter concerns the art of accompaniment, including considerations of the musical qualities desirable in the various members of an orchestra, such as the leader and keyboard player. Quantz also discusses suggested tempos for the different movements in baroque music, including French dance movements. The final chapter considers how to learn to make critical judgements about music and musicians. Quantz examines the characteristics of many types of pieces (particularly those popular in Germany) and then compares the characteristics of the Italian, French, and German styles of musical composition and performance.[3]

- Carl Philipp Emanuel Bach, *Essay on the True Art of Playing Keyboard Instruments*, trans. and ed. William J. Mitchell (New York: W. W. Norton, 1949; London: Cassell, 1951).
C. P. E. Bach's treatise originally appeared in two parts. The first part was initially published in 1753, the second in 1762. Bach was obviously familiar with Quantz's flute treatise. Bach's book contains a wealth of specific information about mid-eighteenth-century performance practices in Berlin. While it was written with the idea of providing enough material to enable a keyboard-player to become a thoroughly accomplished expert in that art, there is much of

---

[3] Additionally, Quantz wrote a lenghty preface to his six duets for two flutes, Op. 2 (1759), translated into English by Edward R. Reilly in 'Further Musical Examples for Quantz's *Versuch*', *Journal of the American Musicological Society*, 17: 2 (1964), 162–5. See also the Quantz *Solfeggi* discussed elsewhere in this chapter.

value to all players. Traverso-players will find the most useful information to be in Part 1 in the chapters on embellishments and performance. Bach intentionally does not discuss the longer embellishments which are not notated, such as cadenzas and the more elaborate interpolations. However, he does give a meticulous exposition of the shorter ornaments, including the appoggiatura, trill, turn, mordent, slide, and snap (*der Schneller*). Bach's explanation of the general usage of embellishments is noteworthy:

They connect and enliven notes and impart stress and accent; they make music pleasing and awaken our close attention. Expression is heightened by them; let a piece be sad, joyful, or otherwise, and they will lend a fitting assistance. Embellishments provide opportunities for fine performance as well as much of its subject matter. They improve mediocre compositions. Without them the best melody is empty and ineffective, the clearest content clouded. (p. 79)

C. P. E. Bach's embellishments represent a viewpoint which incorporates the Italian and French ornaments into the German cultural background. He wrote,

I believe that that style of performance is best, regardless of the instruments, which artfully combines the correctness and brilliance of French ornaments with the suavity of Italian singing. Germans are in a good position to effect such a union so long as they remain free of prejudices. (p. 85)

The chapter on performance is also illuminating for its discussions of rhythm, dissonance, consonance, legato, and overdotting.[4]

- Leopold Mozart, *A Treatise on the Fundamental Principles of Violin Playing*, trans. Editha Knocker (London: Oxford University Press, 1948).
Leopold Mozart's greatest fame in music is as the father of Wolfgang Amadeus Mozart. He was also a composer, a vice-kapellmeister in the service of the Archbishop of Salzburg, a violinist, and a teacher. One of his most important achievements was the writing of a book on how to play the violin and how to teach the art of playing the violin (1756). It is recognized as one of the most valuable performance manuals of the eighteenth century. Although much of the book is devoted to technical matters for violinists, there is also considerable material regarding style which is of value to other instrumentalists. The chapters on appoggiaturas, the trill, and tremolo (vibrato) are indispensable, and the chapter on bowing gives wind players ideas about articulation. Among other

---

[4] As illustrative material for Part 1, Bach composed six keyboard sonatas, and to the 1787 revision of the treatise he added six new sonatas.

topics considered are overdotting, temperament, and dynamics. The following advice by Leopold Mozart is as valid to wind-players as it is to string-players:

Great pains must be taken to obtain evenness of tone; which evenness must be maintained at all times in the changes between strong (*forte*) and weak (*piano*). For *piano* does not consist in simply letting the bow leave the violin and merely slipping it loosely about the strings, which results in a totally different and whistling tone, but the weak must have the same tone quality as the strong, save that it should not sound so loudly to the ear. (p. 100)

● Johann George Tromlitz, *The Virtuoso Flute-Player*.
Tromlitz's instruction book is one of the least well known of the important performance-practice sources of the eighteenth century; however, with the publication of Ardal Powell's new translation, that should change. Tromlitz writes extensively about stylistic matters such as rhythm, tempo, tone, intonation, articulation, affections (ornaments), and free ornamentation. His chapter on rhythm and tempo includes a brief discussion of overdotting. Tempo is established by feeling and recognition of the content of the piece. Tone quality is a matter of taste; for Tromlitz, the model for a beautiful sound is a beautiful singing voice. Regarding intonation, Tromlitz stresses the importance of being able to tune a keyboard instrument; one thus learns how to listen to intervals.

For articulation, he recommends the use of the syllables *ta*, *da*, and *ra* with the *ah* sound, rather than Quantz's *ti*, *di*, *ri* with the *ee* sound, which he feels is too pointed. The shape of the mouth required to make the *ah* sound makes the tone fuller, rounder, and lighter. He discusses patterns of articulation and the importance of understanding stressed and unstressed notes. He also includes a long, detailed chapter on double tonguing.

The ornaments which Tromlitz discusses are vibrato, appoggiatura, termination, slide, turn, mordent, portamento, and trill, among others. All of Tromlitz's ornaments are copiously illustrated and explained in meticulous detail. He also discusses dynamics, including growing louder and softer by introducing crescendo and diminuendo with the signs ◁ and ▷ . The chapter on fermatas and cadenzas includes a number of original cadenzas for one or two instruments, and the chapter on free ornamentation contains an original slow movement illustrating how a simple, unornamented melody may be freely ornamented in several different ways.

Other Primary Sources

● *Solfeggi Pour La Flute Traversiere avec l'enseignement, Par Monsr. Quantz,* modern edition, based on the autograph, ed. Winfried Michel and Hermien Teske (Winterthur: Amadeus, 1978)

This unusual document is a musical notebook which Quantz wrote and kept updated for a private pupil over a period of years. The editors suggest that the anonymous pupil may have been Frederick the Great, although there is no actual proof of that. The material which Quantz assembled consists of short excerpts from works by himself, Hasse, Telemann, C. P. E. Bach, and others. A few works appear in their entirety. The traverso-player will find this notebook of great value as a source of ideas for articulation, for which Quantz has provided an abundance of illustrations.

Another excellent source for style is found in original music of the period. The slow movements of Telemann's Methodical Sonatas for flute and continuo (1728 and 1732) contain both the simplified skeletal version and an ornamented version also by Telemann. These deserve careful study by all players of baroque music. Frederick Neumann has written of them, 'They represent what might well be the most valuable textbook of late Baroque diminution practice, because they strike a happy balance between austerity and luxuriance.'[5] A number of slow movements of traverso sonatas by J. S. Bach are fully written out with ornamentation, a fact of which many flautists are unaware. These movements include the slow movement of the B minor sonata, the opening movement of the E major sonata, and the slow movement of the C major sonata. Players are encouraged to reconstruct theoretical simplified versions of these movements in order to help themselves to perceive the nature of Bach's ornaments.[6]

Among other primary sources of style are the mechanical barrel organs which survive from the baroque and classical eras as well as the contemporary printed instructions for pinning the cylinders. These barrel organs exist in private collections and museums, and occasionally they appear for sale at auctions or from dealers. They are the only true record extant of actual musical performances from pre-gramophone days. While it is true that the pinning may not necessarily represent what a live performance was—the pins, for example, may have become bent—nevertheless, the surviving cylinders can tell us much about relative tempos, note lengths, ornamentation, and rhythm. The most irrefutable evidence for eighteenth-century performance style comes not from a barrel

---

[5] Frederick Neumann, *Ornamentation in Baroque and Post-Baroque Music* (Princeton, NJ: Princeton University Press, 1978), 564.

[6] See John Solum, 'On Perceiving the Written-Out Ornaments in Movements from Bach's Flute Sonatas', *Flutist Quarterly*, 10: 3 (1985).

organ but from the instructions on how to pin the barrel. This appeared in 1778 in Dom Bedos's multi-volume treatise on organ building. The great French organist, Claude Balbastre, was commissioned to write a piece to demonstrate the technique of pinning. While no cylinder exists of the work, Dom Bedos's book contains Balbastre's original piece, Engramelle's notation of what the ornaments should sound like if written out, and charts showing corresponding placement of the pins on a barrel to achieve the composer's desired stylistic details. All of this is explained and illustrated (including a sound recording) in David Fuller's informative booklet, *Mechanical Musical Instruments as a Source for the Study of Notes Inégales*[7]

Secondary Sources

- Arnold Dolmetsch, *The Interpretation of the Music of the XVIIth and XVIIIth Centuries Revealed by Contemporary Evidence.* (London; Novello, 1915, rev. ed. 1946; repr., Seattle: University of Washington Press, 1969).
Although preceded by Edward Dannreuther's *Musical Ornamentation* by twenty years, Dolmetsch's book stood virtually unchallenged for nearly a half-century as a landmark study of baroque performance practices. His approach to the subject is both as a performing musician and as a musicologist. He was no mere pedant; indeed, he was passionately interested in bringing old music to life. He wrote, 'The student should first try and prepare his mind by thoroughly understanding what the Old Masters *felt* about their own music, what impressions they wished to convey, and, generally, what was the *Spirit of their Art*' (p. vii).

    Over half of the book concerns ornamentation, based upon such sources as Simpson, Frescobaldi, Hotteterre, Couperin, Quantz, Leopold Mozart, C. P. E. Bach, and others. Some of Dolmetsch's interpretations of the meaning of his original sources are controversial. For example, part of his chapter on rhythmic alteration has come under critical scrutiny by some scholars who feel that he failed to note that overdotting, as described by Quantz and C. P. E. Bach, should not necessarily be applied retroactively to earlier composers. In general, however, Dolmetsch's book is a remarkable achievement by a major twentieth-century musical visionary.

- Thurston Dart, *The Interpretation of Music* (London: Hutchison's University Library, 1954).

---

[7] Cleveland Heights, Oh.: Divisions, 1979. The address of Divisions is PO Box 18647, Cleveland Heights, OH, USA.

This well-written book is an excellent introduction to some of the general problems of playing early music. Like Dolmetsch, Dart writes from the viewpoint of a practical musician. However, he does not discuss details such as how to play ornaments or what fingerings to use on the keyboard, as does Dolmetsch. Instead, he writes on a somewhat more general level, giving an overview of such topics as sonorities, extemporization, style, and musical notation.

- Robert Donington, *The Interpretation of Early Music* (new version, London: Faber & Faber, 1974; New York: St Martin's Press, 1974).

- Robert Donington, *A Performer's Guide to Baroque Music* (London: Faber & Faber, 1973).

- Robert Donington, *Baroque Music: Style and Performance* (London: Faber Music, 1982).

Donington was an English-born musicologist whose name became a household word in musical circles largely through the publication of *The Interpretation of Early Music*, which originally appeared in 1963. A pupil and admirer of Arnold Dolmetsch, Donington created a standard reference work considerably more extensive than Dolmetsch's book. It is distinguished by its liberal use of selected quotations from the standard treatises to illustrate the author's statements. Some of his conclusions are debatable; he acknowledges his differences with Frederick Neumann on such matters as overdotting and before-the-beat graces, and the early music profession has enthusiastically adopted performing at pitches such as A=430, A=415, and A=392 in spite of Donington's admonition that 'under all ordinary circumstances, therefore, and except for special reasons, we should keep to a$'$=440'.[8]

A Performer's Guide to Baroque Music, a much shorter volume than *Interpretation*, is designed to be of practical help on matters of interest to both musicologist and performer. The two books are intended to be complementary. The *Guide* is a concise survey, not merely a summary of *Interpretation*. Donington calls the *Guide* 'a severely utilitarian course of instruction in the basic know-how of baroque performance'.[9]

Shorter than the other two Donington baroque music books, *Baroque Music: Style and Performance* is appropriately called a handbook since it is succinct and is 'a basic grounding' for students and performers. In his foreward, Donington states that this book 'summarizes the principles of authentic interpretation in baroque music and their practical application in performance'. It represents the

---

[8] *The Interpretation of Early Music*, 511.   [9] Ibid. 34.

distillation of Donington's many years of study of baroque performance practices. Without mentioning Frederick Neumann by name in the text, the book may be seen as Donington's response to Neumann's *Ornamentation in Baroque and Post-Baroque Music* and his other published writings. Donington has accordingly modified some of the viewpoints which he endorsed in his two earlier books, but it does not resolve notable differences of opinion between these two musicologists.

• Frederick Neumann, *Ornamentation in Baroque and Post-Baroque Music* (Princeton, NJ: Princeton University Press, 1978)

• Frederick Neumann, *Ornamentation and Improvisation in Mozart* (Princeton, NJ: Princeton University Press, 1986)
Neumann's books and other published writings have caused considerable discussion and controversy in recent years in musicology and in the field of early music. Neumann sets out to prove erroneous some of the assumed tenets of historical performance practice. In his massive volume on baroque ornamentation, he seeks to demonstrate that the use of ornaments in baroque music was less doctrinaire and much freer than has heretofore been believed. He points out the folly of widespread blanket applications of statements from treatises. For his arguments, Neumann not only draws upon the historical treatises but makes use of a prolific number of examples from baroque and classical music. Especially influential upon current early-music performances are his expositions regarding trills which begin on the principal note, ornaments which occur before the beat, and the use or non-use of overdotting. Of special interest to traverso-players are his insights on specific problems regarding the major works for flute by Bach and Mozart. In general, Neumann pursues his points with fervent determination, so much so that the effectiveness of his books may be somewhat diminished because of it.

• Betty Bang Mather, *Interpretation of French Music from 1675 to 1775 for Woodwind and Other Performers* (New York: McGinnis & Marx, 1973)

• Betty Bang Mather and David Lasocki, *Free Ornamentation in Woodwind Music 1700–1775* (New York: McGinnis & Marx, 1976)

• David Lasocki and Betty Bang Mather, *The Classical Woodwind Cadenza* (New York: McGinnis & Marx, 1978)

• Betty Bang Mather and David Lasocki, *The Art of Preluding 1700–1830 for Flutists, Oboists, Clarinettists and Other Performers* (New York: McGinnis & Marx, 1984)

These four books constitute a series of modestly produced 'workbooks' concerning style for woodwind-players.[10] Betty Bang Mather is one of the first American flautists to have become interested in the traverso and in specific topics related to historical woodwind performance. An Englishman, David Lasocki, became associated with her in studies and projects at the University of Iowa, and their mutual interest in historical performance practices has resulted in several very fruitful collaborations as co-authors. These books, taken as a whole, are uncommonly thoughtful and well organized. In addition to presenting factual material, they function as tutors, leading the player-reader in step-by-step procedures for putting into practice the ideas which are presented.

Many flute-players feel intimidated by French baroque music because the stylistic aspects are so different from Italian-style music and relatively few flute teachers are knowledgeable enough to teach French baroque style. *Interpretation of French Music from 1675 to 1775* systematically illustrates and explains three aspects of French baroque woodwind performance: rhythmic inequality, articulation, and ornamentation. Betty Bang Mather has a great gift for writing, explaining, and organizing her material and for encouraging the reader to experiment and practice in order to develop a first-hand feeling for the style.[11]

Free Ornamentation in Woodwind Music 1700–1775 is an anthology of primary-source musical illustrations of the longer embellishments (as opposed to fixed ornaments) by French, Italian, German, and English composers of the eighteenth century. Most of the illustrations are for the flute although examples for recorder, oboe, and bassoon are also included. The book also helps the reader to perceive the longer embellishments already written out by composers (such as some of the slow movements of Bach flute sonatas) so that the player may perform them with an awareness of their function within the music.[12]

The Classical Woodwind Cadenza not only examines existing original classical cadenzas and attempts to make some general conclusions from them, but also encourages the reader to attempt to compose his or her own cadenzas for classical concertos. This book is an indispensable reference tool for anyone interested in finding typical original classical cadenzas or in writing cadenzas stylistically appropriate for a classical woodwind concerto.

The Art of Preluding 1700–1830 calls attention to an all but lost aspect of historical performance, the often improvised warm-up piece which immediately preceded the performance of a formal piece. The book includes a brief study of the general characteristics of preludes from 1700 to 1830 and a selection of

---

[10] A fifth book by Betty Bang Mather (with the assistance of Dean M. Karns) entitled *Dance Rhythms of the French Baroque: A Handbook for Performance* was published in 1987 by Indiana University Press.

[11] For a book review by John Solum, see *Pro Musica* magazine, 1: 6 (1976).

[12] For a review by John Solum, see *The Consort*, 34 (1978).

preludes by composers such as Hotteterre, Corrette, Devienne, Vanderhagen, and Nicholson. It concludes with a chapter devised to help the reader learn how to improvise preludes; included are instructions from such original tutors as Hotteterre and Corrette as well as general instructions by the authors themselves.

- *The New Grove Dictionary of Music and Musicians*, ed. Stanley Sadie (London: Macmillan, 1980).
  A number of articles on performance style which appear in the *New Grove Dictionary* are of value to players of early music. The contributing authors are all recognized authorities. Among the articles pertinent to early music are 'Articulation', 'Ornamentation' (by Donington), 'Pitch', 'Rhetoric and Music', 'Rhythm', 'Style', 'Temperaments', 'Tempo', and 'Tempo and Expression Marks'.

- *The New Harvard Dictionary of Music*, ed. Don Randel (Cambridge, Mass.: The Belknap Press of Harvard University Press, 1986).
  This one-volume dictionary, comprising nearly six thousand entries contributed by seventy distinguished scholars, contains numerous articles of relevance to early music and style.

- *The New Oxford Companion to Music*, ed. Denis Arnold (Oxford: Oxford University Press, 1983).
  This very useful two-volume mini-encyclopedia of music contains many articles about style concerning historically informed performance. The contributing authors are notable authorities in their respective fields.

Periodicals

Most early-music players keep abreast of current developments on all fronts of early music by reading one or more of the monthy or quarterly periodicals which include articles about early-music style. Perhaps the most influential of these journals is the lavishly produced quarterly *Early Music*, edited by Nicholas Kenyon. Other journals in English include *Music and Letters*, the *Musical Times*, *Journal of Musicology*, *Musical Quarterly*, and the *Journal of the American Musicological Society*. A recent addition to this list is *Historical Performance*, the journal of Early Music America. *Traverso*, a quarterly 'baroque flute newsletter' edited by Ardal Powell and published by Folkers & Powell, contains short articles, reviews, and miscellaneous news exclusively concerning the flauto traverso. The *Galpin Society Journal* and the *Journal of the American Musical Instrument Society* are two annual journals devoted to historical musical instruments. Since instruments are inseparable from considerations of style, they are included here in this list.

The Role of the Performer

When all of the treatises, books, essays, and periodicals have been read, studied, and digested, this still does not provide the early-music performer with a guarantee of a successful performance. Ultimately it is the performer who must conjure up the magic to make a performance meaningful and exciting. Albert Fuller, the distinguished musician and professor at the Juilliard School, stated in a speech in 1986,

When music is made according to books we end up involved in tedious circular arguments. In such arguments, people go round and round claiming that in the exercise of personal art it is possible for some things to be right and others to be wrong, some things to be correct and others incorrect. Surely the concepts of right and wrong, correct or incorrect, have a very dubious place, if any at all, in the world of personal artistic expression . . .[13]

Fuller then stated that our greatest problems lie not so much with our knowledge as with the production of 'touching, moving, thrilling, memorable and persuasive performances' of music. 'In the end,' he continued, 'it isn't so much what or even how much we know, rather, the important thing is what we do with what we know.'

---

[13] Speech delivered at the Oberlin College Conservatory of Music 'Conference on Musical Interpretation: The Influence of Historical Informed Performance', 6–7 Dec. 1986.

9

Sources: Important Solo and Ensemble Repertoire with Recommended Editions

THE transverse flute acquired one of the largest repertoires of any musical instrument in Western art music throughout the eighteenth century and into the early nineteenth. Not only is it extensive—many thousands of works were written for it during this period of approximately a hundred and twenty-five years—but the greatest composers of that era created flute works of enduring beauty. J. S. Bach, Handel, Telemann, C. P. E. Bach, Gluck, Haydn, Mozart, Beethoven, Weber, Schubert, all gave the fruits of their talents to the writing of music involving the transverse flute. In particular, J. S. Bach and Mozart explored many different aspects of the flute and bestowed upon it qualities of dignity, humanity, and nobility which have never been surpassed. These were the finest moments of the flute in terms of its repertoire.

Although all of the above-mentioned composers were born in German-speaking countries, it is of historical interest that the post-Renaissance solo flute repertoire originated in France. This French repertoire was the only real 'school' of flute composition to flourish before Bach began to write specifically for the transverse flute after 1717.

In 1692 in Paris, Marin Marais, employed at the court of Louis XIV, published a volume of six suites called *Pieces en Trio pour les Flutes, Violon, & Dessus de Viole*. The range of the two treble parts indicates that Marais had the recorder in mind as much as the transverse flute when he stated 'flute'. In 1694 and 1700, another musician at the court of Louis XIV, the flautist and composer Michel de la Barre, published two more volumes of *pièces en trio* for either violins, flutes, or oboes. In 1702, de la Barre published a book of five suites for solo flute and figured bass, the first music published specifically for the solo one-keyed conical transverse flute. De la Barre was very much aware of the pioneering aspect of his publication. In the preface he writes, 'these pieces are the first which have appeared for this kind of flute . . .'. It took several years for the momentum to gather, but by 1708 newly published solo music for the one-keyed transverse flute became a regular annual occurrence in France. De la Barre and his colleague, Jacques Hotteterre le Romain, were the two most active composers of traverso music from then until the early 1720s. In 1724 Boismortier began publishing music for transverse flute; his output was vast.

The following selective chronological list of original music for flute by French composers outlines an exceptionally rich musical resource which has been overlooked by many modern flute-players.[1] Although this list does not extend beyond 1729, the activity continued unabated for years and included such distinguished publications as Blavet's six sonatas, Op. 2 (1732), and six sonatas, Op. 3 (1740). This music almost exclusively concerned itself with the dance suite—allemandes, courantes, sarabandes, menuets—rather than with the abstract movements of the Italian style. Even when the title of the work was 'sonate', it was most often a dance suite in disguise, containing allegros and moderatos which are really allemandes and gavottes, for example.

Select List of French Publications of Flute Music 1692–1729

1692	Marin Marais	*Pieces en trio* (2 fl., dessus de viole).
1694	Michel de la Barre	*Pieces en trio* (2 fl., b.c.).
1700	de la Barre	*Pieces en trio*, livre 2.
1702	de la Barre	*Pieces pour la flute traversiere* (comprising 5 suites for fl., b.c.) ('Ces Pièces sont les premiere qui ayent paru pour cette sorte de Flute'—de la Barre).
1703	de la Barre	Second issue of *Pieces pour la flute traversiere*.
1707	de la Barre	*Troisieme livre des trio* (2 fl., b.c.).
	Hotteterre le Romain	*Principes de la flute traversiere*.
1708	Hotteterre	*Pieces pour la flute traversiere*, Op. 2 (3 suites, fl., b.c.; 2 duos, 2 fl.; Echos, fl. unacc.).
1709	de la Barre	*Premiere Suitte* (2 fl.).
	Antoine Dornel	*Livre de simphonies* (6 trios).
1710	de la Barre	*Premier Livre* (new ed. of 1702–3 suites).
	de la Barre	*Deuxieme Livre* (9 suites, fl., b.c.).
	J.-B. Senaillé	*1er livre*, no. 1 (sonata, fl., b.c.).
	de la Barre	*Deuxieme Suite* (2 fl.).
1711	de la Barre	*Troisieme Suite* (2 fl.).
	de la Barre	*Quatrieme Suite* (incl. 5th suite) (2 fl.).
	A. Dornel	4 Suites, Op. 2 (fl., b.c.).

[1] This listing does not include Couperin's chamber music, much of which is suitable for performance with flute, such as the *Concerts royaux* (1714/15), *Les Goûts réunis* (1724), *L'Apothéose de Lully* (1725), and *Les Nations* (1726).

1712	Anne Danican Philidor	*1er livre de pieces* (3 suites, fl., b.c.).

1712 Anne Danican Philidor *1er livre de pieces* (3 suites, fl., b.c.).
      Senaillé   *Deuxième livre*, no. 5 (fl., b.c.).
      Hotteterre   6 Trio sonatas, Op. 3.
      Hotteterre   *Premiere Suitte de Pieces*, Op. 4 (2 dessus).
1713 de la Barre   *Cinquième Livre* (2 suites for 2 fl.).
      A. Dornel   7 sonatas, Op. 3 (six for 2 dessus, b.c., one for 3 dessus).
1714 de la Barre   *Sixième Livre* (2 suites for 2 fl.).
      Anne Danican Philidor *IIe Livre* (fl., b.c.).
1715 Hotteterre   *Deuxième Livre*, Op. 5 (2 suites, 2 sonatas for fl., b.c.).
      Hotteterre   *Premier Livre* (new ed. of 1708 *Pieces pour la flute traversiere*).
1716 François Philidor   *Pieces pour la flute traversiere* (fl., b.c.; one movt. for 2 fl.).
1717 Hotteterre   *Deuxième Suitte*, Op. 6 (2 fl., or 2 fl., b.c.).
      Pierre Philidor   *Premier Oeuvre* (3 suites for 2 fl.; 3 suites for 2 fl., b.c.).
1718 Pierre Philidor   Op. 2 (2 suites for 2 fl.; 2 suites, fl., b.c.).
      Pierre Philidor   Op. 3 (1 suite for 2 fl.; 1 suite, fl., b.c.).
1719 Hotteterre   *L'Art de Preluder.*
1721 de la Barre   *Septième Livre* (2 suites for 2 fl.).
1722 Hotteterre   *Suite*, Op. 8 (for 2 fl., b.c.).
      de la Barre   *Huitième Livre* (2 suites, fl., b.c.).
      de la Barre   *Neufième Livre* (2 sonatas for 2 fl.).
      de la Barre   *Dixième Livre* (2 suites for 2 fl.).
1723 Leclair   Op. 1 (10 sonatas of which 2 may be played by fl. with b.c.).
      Leclair   Op. 2 (incl. 5 sonatas which may be played by fl. with b.c.).
1724 de la Barre   *Unzième Livre* (2 suites for 2 fl.).
      Boismortier   Op. 1, 6 sonatas (2 fl.).
      Boismortier   Op. 2, 6 sonatas (2 fl.).
      Boismortier   Op. 4, trio sonatas (2 fl., b.c.).
      Montéclair   6 Concerts (fl., b.c.) (No. 6 dated 1725).
1725 de la Barre   *Douzième Livre* (2 suites, 2 fl.).
      Boismortier   Op. 3, 6 sonatas (fl., b.c.).
      Boismortier   Op. 6, 6 sonatas (2 fl.).
      Boismortier   Op. 7, 6 sonatas (3 fl.).
      Boismortier   Op. 8, 6 sonatas (2 fl.).

	Boismortier	Op. 9 (sonatas for fl., b.c.).
1726	Caix d'Hervelois	*Pieces* (3 suites for fl., b.c.).
	Naudot	Op. 1, 6 sonatas (fl., b.c.).
	Boismortier	Op. 11, 6 suites (2 fl.).
	Boismortier	Op. 12, trio sonatas (2 fl., b.c.).
	Boismortier	Op. 13, 12 petites sonates (2 fl.).
	Naudot	Op. 2, 6 trio sonatas (2 fl., b.c.).
1727	Corrette	Op. 2, 6 sonatas (2 fl.).
	Naudot	Op. 3, sonatas (2 fl.).
	Boismortier	Op. 15, 6 concertos, (5 fl.).
	Boismortier	Op. 17, 6 suites (2 fl.).
	Boismortier	Op. 19, sonatas (fl., b.c.).
1728	Corrette	Op. 3, 6 concertos (2 fl., b.c.).
	Michel Blavet	Op. 1, 6 sonatas (2 fl.).
	Jean Daniel Braun	Op. 1, 6 sonatas (fl., b.c.).
	Braun	Op. 2, 6 suites (2 fl.).
	Braun	Op. 3, 6 trio sonatas (2 fl., b.c.).
	Naudot	Op. 4, 6 sonatas (fl., b.c.).
	Naudot	Op. 5, 6 sonatas (2 fl.).
	Boismortier	Op. 21, 6 concertos (fl., 2 vn., b.c.).
	Boismortier	Op. 22, diverse pieces (fl. unacc.).
1729	Boismortier	Op. 24, 6 concertos (fl., 2 vn., b.c.).
	Boismortier	Op. 25, 6 sonatas (2 fl.).

From 1730 to 1742, Boismortier published the following opuses of music for flute: 27, 28, 29, 30, 33, 34, 35, 37, 38, 39, 41, 42, 44, 45, 46, 47, 49, 51, 52, 53, 56, 57, 64, 65, 69, 73, 74, 75, 78, 80, 85, 87, 90, 91.

Meanwhile, in Germany at the beginning of the eighteenth century there was no strong tradition of writing for the transverse flute. Buxtehude, Erlebach, Johann Caspar Ferdinand Fischer, Pachelbel, Theile, Walther, Strungk, Biber, Birkenstock, Pisendel, Krieger, Rosenmüller, Muffat, Kusser, and Mayr had all ignored the transverse flute. Pez and Pepusch are two of the most prominent Germans who did write for the traverso. Before 1717, all of J. S. Bach's compositions involving the 'flute' had been composed for the recorder. It was only after 1717, when he moved to Köthen, that he began writing specifically for the transverse flute. And how he wrote for it! He responded almost instantly to the stimulus of the traverso when he first became exposed to it and quickly became a pioneer in its use. Without any flute-writing tradition on which to build—it is conceivable that he may have seen copies of the published French music but there is no factual evidence to confirm this—he started writing for the traverso on a very high level. The tradition in his own writing which most influenced his flute works was his string writing, especially his solo violin works. In the next thirty years, he was to create the greatest body of flute music ever written by any major composer. (Historically speaking, Mozart was his only rival in this regard.) His flute music involves as many as thirteen solo or chamber pieces (of which the authenticity of several has been questioned) plus important solo parts in the B minor Mass, the St John Passion, the St Matthew Passion, the Magnificat, and many of his cantatas, both sacred and secular.

In his instrumental music, Bach frequently wrote in sets of six, such as his six French suites, six English suites, six sonatas for violin and harpsichord, six sonatas and partitas for solo violin, etc. However, such was not the case with the flute sonatas. Modern research has shown that the sonatas were written over many years, interspersed with the other solo works which he wrote involving the flute. This shatters the nineteenth-century notion that Bach wrote almost all of his flute music at Köthen between the years 1717–23.

Chronology of Bach's Flute Works[2]

*c.*1718	Partita in A minor, BWV 1013.
1719–21	Fifth Brandenburg Concerto, BWV 1050.
*c.*1724	Sonata in E minor, BWV 1034.
1729–41	Triple Concerto in A minor, BWV 1044.
*c.*1730–4	Sonata in E flat major, BWV 1031.
*c.*1731	Sonata in C major, BWV 1033.
1732–5	Trio in G major (fl., vn., b.c.), BWV 1038.
*c.*1736	Sonata in B minor, BWV 1030.
*c.*1736	Sonata in A major, BWV 1032.
1736–41	Sonata in G major (2 fl., b.c.), BWV 1039.
*c.*1738–9	Ouverture in B minor, BWV 1067.
1741	Sonata in E major, BWV 1035.
1747	Musical Offering, BWV 1079.

The question of authenticity that has been raised regarding several of these works became an issue when the Neue Bach Ausgabe (1963) excluded on stylistic grounds the Sonata in C major, BWV 1033, and the Sonata in E flat

---

[2] The following general dating has been largely proposed by Prof. Robert L. Marshall. (See 'J. S. Bach's Compositions for Solo Flute: A Reconsideration of their Authenticity and Chronology', *Journal of the American Musicological Society*, 32: 3 (1979), repr. in Marshall, *The Music of Johann Sebastian Bach: The Sources, the Style, the Significance* (New York: Schirmer Books, 1989), 201–25). Except for the first two works (which were written in Köthen), the rest are dated here as given in Prof. Christoph Wolff's article 'Bach's Leipzig Chamber Music', *Early Music*, 13: 2 (1985), 169. Some of the Leipzig works may have existed in other, earlier versions in the Köthen period. The date of *c.*1718 for the A minor Partita is suggested by Prof. Marshall.

major, BWV 1031. However, in 1979 the noted American Bach scholar, Professor Robert L. Marshall, published an article in which he proposed that rightfully belonging to Bach's *œuvre* are the E flat major and C major sonatas, the latter perhaps having been originally conceived as an unaccompanied flute work.[3] Marshall suggests that J. S. Bach gave his youthful son, C. P. E. Bach, a composition lesson to construct a bass line to the C major sonata. In any case, the work survives in a manuscript in the hand of C. P. E. Bach entitled 'Sonata a Traversa e continuo di Joh. Seb. Bach'. The Sonata in E flat major survives in two mid-eighteenth-century manuscripts, one of which bears the title in the hand of C. P. E. Bach: 'Es d[ur] Trio Fürs obligate Clavier u. die Flöte Von J. S. Bach'. The other copy, partly in the hand of the Bach copiest, C. F. Penzel, also attributes the work to J. S. Bach. Marshall also proposes that the Sonata in G minor, BWV 1020, is not by J. S. Bach but by C. P. E. Bach and is for violin and obbligato harpsichord. This agrees with an entry in the 1763 Breitkopf Catalogue of Music in Manuscript, where it is listed as a sonata for violin and obbligato harpsichord by C. P. E. Bach, with an incipit of the work. The arguments put forth in print by modern Bach scholars regarding authenticity of certain works should not intimidate traverso-players. Regardless of who wrote them, these are fine eighteenth-century solo works for flute, and scarcely a note has been changed in them through all of the musicological discourse.

　It is supremely rewarding to study and play Bach's flute works on the traverso. The articulations, phraseology, and distinctive colours of the different notes of the scale on the traverso notably enhance the meaning and interest of these pieces. While technically challenging, Bach's works for solo traverso are by no means impossible and, in fact, are no more difficult for a traverso-player than the Ibert Concerto or Prokofiev Sonata are to modern Boehm-system flute-players.

　Bach's principal rivals in Germany as composers of solo and chamber works for flute were Georg Philipp Telemann and Carl Philipp Emanuel Bach. In the space of about a dozen years, Telemann produced at least a dozen major publications involving flute, usually in sets of six or twelve pieces. (By contrast, J. S. Bach's works for flute survive only in manuscript copies, except for the Musical Offering, which was engraved under Bach's supervision as a musical homage to Frederick the Great.)

Major Telemann Publications Involving Flute

1727	Six sonatas, Op. 2 (2 fl.).
1728–9	*Der getreue Music-Meister.*

[3] See Marshall, 'J. S. Bach's Compositions for Solo Flute', 468.

1728	Methodical sonatas, Op. 13 (6 sonatas, fl., b.c.).
1730	Six quartets (fl., vn., gamba, b.c.) ('Paris').
*c.*1732	Twelve Fantasias (fl. unacc.).
1732	Methodical sonatas (6 additional, fl., b.c.).
1733	*Musique de table* (sonatas, concertos, quartets, etc.).
1734	Twelve solos (fl. or vn., b.c.).
1734	Six concerts and six suites (fl., hpd. obbl./fl., vc., hpd. obbl./fl., vn., vc./fl., vn., b.c.).
1738	Six canonic sonatas, Op. 5 (2 fl.).
1738	Six quartets (fl., vn., gamba, b.c.) ('Paris', 2nd set) (J. S. Bach was a subscriber to this edn.).
1739–40	*Essercizii musici* (various combinations).

Telemann's music for flute is always beautifully crafted and shows a special insight into the nature and spirit of the traverso. It is impossible here to discuss all of his music for flute. To single out two genres as examples, the twelve Fantasias for solo flute (only made available in a modern edition as recently as 1955) are among the gems of the flute repertoire of the baroque age. Telemann gave them his greatest skill, wit, and imagination. He was also a peerless composer of duos for two flutes without bass, his output comprising a total of twenty-four sonatas contained in a set of six in his published Op. 2, six in Op. 5, and two further sets which were published for the first time in 1955.

Only two of Handel's sonatas for traverso and continuo are of unquestioned authenticity, those being the sonata in E minor, Op. 1 No. 1a (the autograph of which is in the British Library) and the recently-discovered Sonata in D major.[4] Three other Handel traverso sonatas from Op. 1 (No. 1b in E minor, No. 5 in G major, and No. 9 in B minor) are all transpositions of sonatas written for violin, oboe, and recorder, respectively. Although Handel may have had some involvement with the transpositions, the publisher, Walsh, was probably the transcriber. Among the very greatest trio sonatas ever written for the flute are two from Handel's Op. 2. No. 1 in B minor is a later version of a C minor trio sonata, and no. 4 in F major is the other. In each case, the traverso is the top voice and the violin plays second.

Vivaldi wrote a large number of sonatas, concertos, and chamber works involving the traverso. The finest of these are the six concertos which he assembled as Op. 10 for publication by Le Cene in Amsterdam in about 1729.[5]

---

[4] See David Lasocki and Terence Best, 'A New Flute Sonata by Handel', *Early Music*, 9: 3 (1981), and Terence Best, 'Handel's Chamber Music: Sources, Chronology and Authenticity', *Early Music*, 13: 4 (1985).
[5] These concertos have been assigned the numbers RV428, RV433, RV435, RV437, RV439, and RV442 by Peter Ryom in his index, *Répertoire des Œuvres d'Antonio Vivaldi* (Copenhagen: Engstrom & Sodring, 1986).

These works are, for the most part, Vivaldi's own reworkings of earlier chamber concertos involving a variety of instruments. These delightful works are among the first concertos ever published for the transverse flute.[6] They are brimming with imagination, invention, and charm. What other flute concerto contains a movement with the flute solo playing a cadenza at the beginning, rather than at the end, as does the Concerto in D major, 'Il Gardellino', Op. 10 No. 3?

Carl Philipp Emanuel Bach wrote prolifically and magnificently for the flute. His works deserve closer attention by flautists; many of his fine works are rarely encountered in performance. Perhaps his most frequently played flute work is the Sonata in A minor for unaccompanied flute (Helm 562), written in 1747 and published in 1763 in an anthology called *Musikalisches Mancherley*. The correct order of movements is Poco adagio, Allegro 2/4, Allegro 3/8. Some modern editions erroneously place the Poco adagio movement between the two Allegro movements. Among C. P. E. Bach's most substantial chamber works are his three quartets (really trios) for flute, viola, and fortepiano (H. 537–9), composed in the last year of his life, 1788. Also of major importance in the flute repertoire are his five sonatas for flute and cembalo obbligato (H. 505–6, 508–9, 515) and eleven sonatas for flute and figured bass (H. 548, 550–6, 560–1, 564) which encompass a span of more than fifty years of his creative life.

C. P. E. Bach's five concertos for flute and strings include four (in A minor, B flat major, A major, and G major, H. 431, 435, 438, 445, respectively) which date from the 1750s and which were all composed originally as keyboard concertos, later arranged by the composer as flute concertos. (At the time, C. P. E. Bach was employed as a court musician to Frederick the Great.) These four concertos are technically among the most challenging works in the traverso repertoire; the virtuoso solo parts frequently contain arpeggiated passages which are unidiomatic for the traverso and are much more characteristic of keyboard writing. The fifth concerto, in D minor (H. 484.1), also exists in a version for keyboard (H. 425, 1747). It is much more gratefully written for the traverso than the other four C. P. E. Bach concertos. In spite of its flute-like qualities, however, the editors of the C. P. E. Bach complete works edition (Oxford University Press) do not accept the flute version as an authentic arrangement, largely because it is not listed in the C. P. E. Bach *Nachlass-Verzeichnis*[7] In

---

[6] Robert Woodcock's three concertos for German flute were published in London by Walsh in 1727.

[7] Alfred Wotquenne omitted the flute version from his 1905 C. P. E. Bach thematic catalogue, and Rachel Wade lists it as 'an arrangement of questionable authenticity' in her book, *The Keyboard Concertos of Carl Philipp Emanuel Bach* (Ann Arbor, Mich.: UMI Research Press, 1981). It is listed as 'doubtful' in E. Eugene Helm's *Thematic Catalogue of the Works of Carl Philipp Emanuel Bach* (New Haven, Conn.: Yale University Press, 1989).

making their determination, however, the complete works editors did not know that extensive excerpts from the concerto were included by Quantz in his recently discovered workbook known as *Solfeggi* (see Chapter 8).[8] Moreover, the differences between the keyboard and flute versions not only show the necessary rewriting of the solo part, but extensive alterations to the tutti passages as well. Who but C. P. E. Bach would have cared about rewriting the tutti passages? Clearly, more research needs to be done on this excellent concerto.

Other well-known concertos for flute which originated at the court of Frederick the Great are by the flute-playing King himself, Franz Benda, and Quantz. The latter composed at least three hundred concertos, the majority of which remain unpublished and may be found in manuscript in the Deutsche Staatsbibliothek in Berlin.

In the decade of 1760–70, a number of fine early classical concertos were written for flute. Concertos by Johann Christian Bach, Dittersdorf, Grétry, Piccinni, Gluck, and two by Michael Haydn constitute a group of splendid works which are important as precursors to Mozart's concertos of the next decade. Averaging between twelve and fourteen minutes in duration, most of them are scored for an accompanying orchestra of strings and two horns.

The Grétry Concerto is one of the wittiest concertos ever written for flute. It was commissioned by Lord Abingdon, who later patronized the Bach–Abel concerts in London and befriended Haydn. The Gluck Concerto is of exceptional beauty. Andrew Porter, music critic of the *New Yorker*, has described it as a 'cool, poised' work and brings attention to 'its boldness (there is brave writing for the two horns that join the string band)' and 'its grace'.[9] The three cadenzas which are found in the source manuscript of this concerto are outstanding examples of classical flute cadenzas. In fact, Betty Bang Mather considers them to be the finest cadenzas which she has found for any woodwind concerto in the eighteenth century.[10] The so-called Joseph Haydn Flute Concerto is actually by Leopold Hoffmann, although there is a lost Haydn

---

[8] *Solfeggi Pour La Flute Traversiere avec l'enseignement, Par Mons.ʳ Quatz*, a manuscript in the Royal Library in Copenhagen, has been published by Winfried Michel and Hermien Teske (Winterthur: Amadeus, 1978). The editors suggest that the manuscript originated over a period of years, giving 1728 to 1742 as a possible inclusive time span. The excerpts from the D minor Concerto appear on p. 40 of the published edition. Quantz's caption is 'Allᵒ di molto Concerto di Bach'. Editors Michel and Teske are in error in attributing this to Wilhelm Friedemann Bach, as listed in their Register of Composers, p. 95. There is no evidence that W. F. Bach ever wrote a flute concerto, and Quantz's extensive musical quotations are clearly from the last movement of the C. P. E. Bach D minor Concerto.

[9] *New Yorker*, 14 July 1980, p. 89.

[10] Noted in personal correspondence with the author. The cadenzas are printed in the Amadeus edition of the concerto, ed. Rien de Reede.

Flute Concerto of *c.*1761–5 the incipit of which appears in Haydn's own thematic catalogue:[11]

The Mannheim school of composers produced dozens of additional flute concertos during the decades of 1750 to 1780. However, the modest talents of Anton, Johann and Carl Stamitz, Ignaz Holzbauer, Antonin Filtz, Franz Xaver Richter, Carlo Giuseppe Toeschi, and Christian Cannabich lacked the originality or imagination to compose works of any great distinction or personality.

Mozart's works for flute constitute another summit of the traverso repertoire. Six of the works—the Concertos in G major and D major, K. 313 and 314, the Andante, K. 315, and the Quartets for flute, violin, viola, and cello, K. 285, 285a, and 285b—are the result of a commission in 1777 by Ferdinand Dejean in Mannheim.[12] The Flute and Harp Concerto, K. 299, was commissioned in 1778 by the Duc de Guines while Mozart was in Paris. It is of especial interest to traverso-players inasmuch as in each movement the flute is scored as low as c′. This is proof that the Duc de Guines played a traverso with multiple keys, including a foot piece with keys for c♯′ and c′. It was presumably while he was serving as French envoy to Britain that he acquired a six-keyed traverso, a type of flute which had already become fashionable in England by 1778. The last major work for flute by Mozart is the Quartet in A major, K. 298, composed in Vienna in 1786. Mozart's youthful six sonatas, K. 10–15, written when he was 8 years old, are really violin pieces, even though the flute is mentioned on the

---

[11] See Haydn's Entwurf-Katalog, p. 19, and the Elssler Haydn Verzeichnis, p. 22. Robbins Landon has told the author that he thinks there is a 5% chance that the lost concerto may yet be found.

[12] The author is indebted to Carleton Sprague Smith for bringing to his attention recent research on Dejean. The results of this research are found in an article by Frank Lequin, 'Mozart's " . . . rarer Mann"', *Mitteilungen der Internationalen Stiftung Mozarteum*, 29: double vol. 1–2 (1981). According to Lequin's article, Ferdinand Dejean was christened in Bonn on 9 Oct. 1731. Nothing else is known of his early life. He joined the United East India Co. in 1758 as a physician and arrived in Batavia (now Jakarta, Java) in 1759. In 1767 he was discharged at his own request, arriving back in Amsterdam in 1768. Thereafter, it seems that he had an independent income to the end of his life. Dejean, not being a doctor of medicine but rather 'just a surgeon', entered Leiden University in 1769. In 1773 he received his doctorates in philosophy and liberal arts as well as medicine. His wife died in 1773, after which Dejean embarked on extensive travels around Europe. He settled in Mannheim briefly in 1777, where he met Mozart. A notarial deed exists which confirms that Dejean was in Mannheim on 14 Feb. 1778, the same day on which Mozart wrote to his father mentioning Dejean's presence there. Later, Dejean settled in Vienna, where he published in Latin (1792–4) an elaborate, 4-vol. commentary on a work on pathology by his former teacher, Gaubius. Of the 110 dedicatees mentioned in these volumes, many of them were friends of Mozart or were historically associated with him. There is no actual evidence that Dejean and Mozart associated with each other in Vienna. Dejean died in Vienna on 23 Feb. 1797. In an official inventory of his possessions at his death, a transverse flute and sheet music are listed. (The above factual information was developed by Frank Lequin from materials in the archives of the Verenigde Oost-Indische Compagnie.)

title-page. As Frans Vester has pointed out, to perform these on the flute, radical transcription is required.[13] More plausible as a flute and keyboard work by Mozart is the Sonata in G major, K. 301, also composed in Mannheim in 1778 and which was begun by Mozart as a flute sonata but completed as a violin sonata. This is an attractive work for which flautists can rightfully stake at least a partial claim.[14]

Arrangements for flute of works originally written for other instruments were commonly made in the eighteenth and nineteenth centuries, and some of them are idiomatic for the traverso. Mozart's Rondo in C major, K. 373, for violin and orchestra was arranged for flute, being transposed to the key of D. It was thus published in 1801. August Eberhard Müller arranged Joseph Haydn's string quartet, Op. 77 No. 1 (omitting the minuet) for flute and piano, and it was published in this version in 1803. It is one of the finest and most frequently played of all arrangements for flute. Six quartets for flute, violin, viola, and cello, Op. 5, by Haydn are probably anonymous transcriptions of divertimenti by Haydn. Two of these works (Hob. II: 1 and Hob. II: 11) appear in Haydn's Entwurf Catalogue as works for 2 violins, flute, oboe, cello, and bass. The versions for flute, violin, viola, and cello are excellent.

Although Joseph Haydn was a generation older than Mozart, his authenticated chamber works with flute postdate Mozart's flute works with the exception of the A major Quartet, K. 298.[15] Haydn's first major set of unquestionably authentic flute chamber works is a book of six divertimenti for flute, violin, and cello, published by Forster, London, in 1784 (Hob. IV: 6–11). To compose these modest but exquisite trios, Haydn found inspiration in a number of his own earlier works, including *Il Mondo della Luna, Philemon und Baucis, La Vera Costanza*, and his baryton trios numbers 97 and 98. In 1790 John Bland in London published three trios for piano, flute and cello (Hob. XV: 15–17). The G major trio is Haydn's finest surviving work for flute and one of the outstanding classical works for flute. The D major trio (Hob. XV: 16) is a curious work. Charles Rosen has even suggested that it may not be by Joseph Haydn but 'probably' by his brother Michael.[16] Four trios by Haydn for two flutes and cello, called the 'London' Trios (Hob. IV: 1–4) were written in the 1790s when Haydn was in London. These chamber music gems are far from inconsequen-

---

[13] See Frans Vester, *Flute Music of the 18th Century* (Monteux: Musica Rara, 1985), 322.

[14] Ibid. 322. See also the preface by Eduard Reeser to the Bärenreiter ed. of Mozart's Sonatas for Piano and Violin, K. 301–6, 296, 378 (Bärenreiter 4774) and Ricarda Bröhl, 'Die Flötensonaten Wolfgang Amadeus Mozarts', *Tibia*, 3 (1979).

[15] See Carleton Sprague Smith, 'Haydn's Chamber Music and the Flute', *Musical Quarterly*, 19: 3 and 4 (1933).

[16] See Charles Rosen, *The Classical Style* (New York, W. W. Norton, 1971), 354, and Alan Tyson, 'Haydn and Two Stolen Trios', *Music Review*, 22 (1961).

tial; H. C. Robbins Landon has written of their 'charm, vitality and technical mastery' and, with regard to Haydn's powers as a composer at this time, he writes that these trios are works of 'music's most experienced craftsman . . . it is astonishing to see with what care Haydn worked on these little Divertimenti'.[17] When these works were written, Mozart had died, Beethoven was not yet a mature composer, and Haydn was the greatest living composer. The second of these trios was written for Lord Abingdon, the same Englishman for whom Grétry wrote his Flute Concerto in 1765. The second flute part in the third trio descends to low c#', which suggests that one of the amateurs for whom Haydn wrote this trio had a traverso with an extended foot piece.

Beethoven's works involving the flute do not represent the composer at his best. The Trio in G major for flute, bassoon, and piano was written in 1786 in Bonn for the family of Count von Westerholt-Gysenberg. A son, Count Wilhelm, was the flautist. The trio fulfils its obligations to each of the three instruments involved by giving them ample opportunity to shine, including a finale with the requisite set of variations. The Allegro and Menuetto for two flutes (1792) is another conventional domestic piece, written for his friend, J. M. Degenharth, shortly before Beethoven moved from Bonn to Vienna. Beethoven's finest work for flute is his Serenade in D major, Op. 25, for flute, violin, and viola, composed in 1801 and published in 1802. The work is interesting in being scored for two soprano instruments and an alto; Beethoven demonstrates his skill at writing for a trio without a standard bass instrument. Although the work is essentially 'classical', we know we are in the nineteenth century because of the high tessitura of the flute (a fact which Boehm flute-players may not notice but which any traverso-player will immediately detect). The work requires virtuosity and musicianship as much from the violinist and the violist as from the flautist.

During three decades of Beethoven's gradual emergence as a truly great composer, dozens of flute concertos were published to satisfy the demands of professional flautists as well as amateurs. Following is a chronological list of some of the most important concertos published between 1782 and 1814, excluding completely any of the thirty or more flute concertos which the prolific Franz Hoffmeister composed and published during this time.

Date of publication	City of publication	Composer and Work
1782	Paris	Devienne, Concerto No. 1 in D major.
1783	Paris	Devienne, Concerto No. 2 in D major.

[17] See H. C. Robbins Landon, *Haydn in England 1791–1794* (Bloomington, Ind.: Indiana University Press, 1976), 407.

1784	Paris	Devienne, Concerto No. 3 in G major.
1785	Paris	Cambini, Concerto in D major, Op. 37 No. 1.
1785	Paris	Cambini, Concerto in G major, Op. 37 No. 2.
*c.*1789	Paris	Devienne, Concerto No. 4 in G major.
*c.*1792	Paris	Devienne, Concerto No. 5 in G major.
1794	Offenbach	Devienne, Concerto No. 6 in D major.
*c.*1793–4	Paris	Devienne, Concerto No. 7 in E minor.
*c.*1794	Paris	Devienne, Concerto No. 8 in G major.
1793	Paris	Devienne, Concerto No. 9 in E minor.
1799	Paris, Offenbach, Vienna, Rotterdam	Pleyel, Concerto in C major (composed 1797).
1802	Paris	Devienne, Concerto No. 10 in D major.
1803	Paris, Bonn	Cimarosa, Concertante in G major for 2 flutes (composed 1793).
*c.*1806	Leipzig	Danzi, Concerto No. 1 in G major, Op. 30.
*c.*1806	Leipzig	Danzi, Concerto No. 2 in D minor, Op. 31.
*c.*1806	Offenbach	Devienne, Concerto No. 11 in B minor.
*c.*1806	Offenbach	Devienne, Concerto No. 12 in A major.
1814	Leipzig	Danzi, Concerto No. 3 in D minor, Op. 42.
1814	Leipzig	Danzi, Concerto No. 4 in D major, Op. 43.

Not even the French Revolution could ruffle the superficial charm of these concertos, with their predictable harmonies, routine procedures, and excessively long technical displays (albeit well suited to the flute). Certainly the most popular and perhaps the most successful of the above works is the Cimarosa Concertante, which seems to reflect the sunshine of Italy with its engaging melodies and carefree disposition. Franz Danzi is important in the history of music as a teacher, friend, and confidant of Carl Maria von Weber. Danzi's flute concertos are interesting historically for their expanded orchestrations. The norm for flute concertos from the 1770s had been an orchestra of two oboes, two horns, and strings. Cimarosa's Concertante for two flutes added a bassoon to the orchestra—a bassoon with its own independent line, not merely a doubling of the basses. Danzi's first flute concerto added a second bassoon, and the remaining three Danzi concertos (Op. 31, 42, and 43) added two trumpets and timpani to the accompanying three pairs of oboes, horns, and bassoons (plus, of course, the strings). It is the more colourful role of the orchestra, rather than any distinguishing achievement of the music *per se*, which gives the Danzi concertos their somewhat special place in the overall spectrum of the flute repertoire.

Johann Nepomuk Hummel, a pupil of Mozart, composed three flute–piano sonatas of substance and interest. The G major Sonata offers a choice of two slow movements. Its last movement, a rondo, includes a theme which imitates the theme of the refrain of the rondo finale of Mozart's 'Coronation' Piano Concerto, K. 537:[18]

Hummel

Mozart

Another theme is a quotation from Mozart's *Exsultate, Jubilate*, K. 165:

Hummel

Mozart

These references to Mozart were perhaps Hummel's homage to him, since this sonata was written in 1792, one year after Mozart's death. This work is still very much of the eighteenth century and is easily played on the one-keyed traverso. The A major Sonata, written *c.*1814, requires a multi-keyed flute with its range from c♯' to a'''. The general style of writing, however, is what might be termed neo-Haydnesque, evoking the style of Haydn almost self-consciously,

[18] The author is indebted to Igor Kipnis for noting this similarity.

as if Hummel were trying to compose in a 'classical' style appropriate for the late eighteenth century. At the same time, the sonata does not belie its nineteenth-century origins. The best known of Hummel's flute sonatas is the D major Sonata, Op. 50, composed between 1810 and 1815. This is a work for a six- or eight-keyed flute. The third movement rondo of this sonata also contains a musical reference to Mozart, which is sometimes called Mozart's motto, inasmuch as this theme appears in his Symphony No. 33 (first movement), Symphony No. 41 (Finale), and the F major Mass of 1774.

Another excellent sonata from this time (1814) is the E flat major Sonata, Op. 169, of Ferdinand Ries, who was a friend and pupil of Beethoven. The influence of Beethoven may be heard throughout this well-crafted piece. Friedrich Kuhlau's many sonatas and chamber works with flute are worthy of attention. His Sonata in E minor, Op. 71, is one of his greatest works for the flute–piano combination; the piece is conceived on unusually broad outlines and is big in every sense of the word. Similar mastery in handling broad-scaled musical forms may be found in his three quintets for flute and string quartet, Op. 51 (the quartet consisting of one violin, two violas, and one cello).

One of the finest chamber music works with flute from the entire nineteenth century is Carl Maria von Weber's Trio in G minor, Op. 63 (1819) for flute, cello, and piano. John Warrack has called this 'one of Weber's strangest and most affecting works, and the one which exercises him most in keeping a classically based formal control over very diverse material'.[19]

The last solo work to be considered in this whirlwind survey of repertoire for the transverse flute is Schubert's Introduction and Variations on 'Trockne Blumen', Op. 160 (1824). In comparison with others that were composed for solo flute during the nineteenth century, this is a superior piece. However, compared with Schubert's other works in variation form, it falls short of his own standards.[20] Of interest to flautists is the fact that Schubert scored the flute to low b in Variation VI. (Schubert had first composed, but rejected, a version of Variation V which required the flautist to play low b no less than twelve times!)[21]

Schubert's Variations is the last major flute work in the first half of the nineteenth century to have been written by a major composer. As the flute underwent its transformation from a simple-system wooden or ivory instrument with six or eight keys to a cylindrical metal tube with a complex system of keys, the great composers avoided the flute as a solo instrument for almost the entire remainder of the century. (Only Brahms in his four symphonies sought out the

---

[19] John Warrack, *Carl Maria von Weber* (New York: Macmillan, 1968), 192.
[20] See Maurice J. E. Brown, *Schubert's Variations* (London: Macmillan, 1954), 53–7.
[21] Both the Bärenreiter and Schott/Universal edns. include the early version of Variation V.

quality of nobility in the flute which Bach, Handel, Gluck, Mozart, and a few others had expressed so compellingly over a century before.) It is ironic that it was a German, Theobald Boehm, who largely invented the new machine-age flute; but it was the French who found the style and spirit of the new flute. Debussy's *Prélude à l'après-midi d'un faune* (1892–4) ushered in a new era for the flute, recognizing heretofore latent tonal colours in the new instrument which was so radically different from the one which had inspired the greatest composers of the eighteenth and early nineteenth centuries.

Recommended Editions

In playing the early flute, it is essential to read from accurate, 'clean' editions of the music.[22] Many of the editions readily available on the shelves in most music shops are so unscholarly, so arbitrarily 'edited' with the personal interpretive markings of the editor, that it is impossible to ascertain what the composer might have originally written. Since players of early music take the trouble to acquire historical instruments and to learn something about the style and techniques of playing on them, is it too much to ask the same players to seek out the composer's original text? Of course, the ideal text is either the composer's autograph manuscript or an edition printed under the direction of the composer. Fortunately, more of these are becoming available in faithful reproductions. Correctly edited modern editions should clearly indicate what is original and what are editorial additions. If more than one original source is used, editorial commentary should explain the possible choices when differences between texts occur.

By 'text' is meant not merely the notes, but also articulations, dynamics, and figures for the bass. Editions from the latter part of the nineteenth century and from much of the twentieth frequently have articulations and dynamics added which are contrary to what is suitable for the original instrument or what is known about historical use of articulation or dynamics. In the eighteenth century, the player was in partnership with the composer in creating many aspects of performance. The printed page was frequently devoid of any markings for dynamics or articulations, and the performer was expected to add them. As Robert Donington has written, 'The baroque habit was few expression marks, but plenty of expression.'[23] The traverso-player especially should welcome the opportunity to create dynamics which can accommodate the natural characteristics of the instrument. The veiled and darker colours of the

---

[22] For a good general discussion of modern edns., see Thurston Dart, *The Interpretation of Music* (London: Hutchinson's University Library, 1954), 18–28.

[23] Robert Donington, *A Performer's Guide to Baroque Music* (London: Faber & Faber, 1973), 26.

forked fingerings can be turned to advantage by judiciously planning the dynamic scheme.

Recommended Editions: Facsimile

In the past few years, a veritable industry has arisen in the production of facsimile editions of music for scholars, libraries, and performers. An American dealer, James A. Yeager, whose company, Early Music Facsimiles, sells facsimile editions from many sources, lists editions from over fifty publishers in his 1988 catalogue.[24] One of the most universally admired of all facsimile publishers is Studio per Edizioni Scelte, which produces indispensable facsimiles of many of the early eighteenth-century French editions, among others. Included in this distinguished collection are flute works by Blavet, Boismortier, Braun, de la Barre, De Lusse, Devienne, Dornel, Hotteterre, Leclair, Mahaut, Marais, Naudot, Philidor (Pierre, Anne Danican, and François), and others.

Recommended Editions: Modern

C. P. E. Bach	Sonata in A minor for fl. unacc. (Amadeus BP 675 and Universal Wien 18027 both include a facsimile of the original edition of 1763; Deutscher Ricordi).
	Sonatas in D, E, G, and G (Brietkopf EB 8474/75).
	Concerto in A minor (Eulenburg).
	Concerto in B flat major (Musica Rara).
	Concerto in A major (Eulenburg).
	Concerto in G major (Musica Rara).
	Concerto in D minor (Kunzelmann).
	Quartets [Trios] in A, D, and G, for fl., va., pf. (Nagels 222–4).
J. C. Bach	Concerto in D major (Universal Zürich 12770; a facsimile of the autograph is found in the Collected Works of Johann Christian Bach, Vol. 36, Garland Publishing).
J. S. Bach	Partita in A minor for fl. unacc. (Amadeus BP 2460 includes a facsimile of the source MS; Bärenreiter 4401; Henle; Universal Wien 18023 includes the C major sonata as a solo work; Breitkopf 8550).
	Sonatas in B minor, A major, E minor, E major (Bärenreiter 4402; Henle; Peters 4461a/b also includes the sonatas in C major and E flat major; Universal Wien 17294/17295).

---

[24] The address of Early Music Facsimiles is PO Box 711, Columbus, Ohio 43216, USA.

	Sonata in A major (Hänssler, completion by Michael Marissen; Oxford, completion by Samuel Baron).
	Sonatas in C major, E flat major, G minor (Bärenreiter 4418; Henle).
	Ouverture (Suite) No. 2 in B minor (Peters 4417).
	Trio Sonata in C minor (Musical Offering) for fl., vn., b.c. (Henle; Bärenreiter).
	Concerto in A minor for fl., vn., hpd. (Breitkopf 4328; Peters 9383).
	Trio Sonata in G major for fl., vn., b.c. (Peters 4203b).
	Brandenburg Concerto No. 5 (Bärenreiter 5112, the separate parts of which have been edited without indication; be sure to compare with the Bärenreiter score, which is correct).
Beethoven	Allegro and Menuetto for 2 fl. (Editio Musica Budapest).
	Serenade in D major, Op. 25, for fl., vn., va. (Breitkopf & Härtel; Henle).
Cimarosa	Concerto [Concertante] in G major for 2 fl. (Bote & Bock).
Danzi	Concerto No. 1 in G major, Op. 30 (Heinrichshofen).
	Concerto No. 2 in D minor, Op. 31 (Heinrichshoften).
	Concerto No. 3 in D minor, Op. 42 (Willy Müller).
	Concerto No. 4 in D major, Op. 43 (Eulenburg GM 144).
	Sonatine in D major for fl., pf. (Hofmeister; Schott 6191).
de la Barre	Pieces pour la flute traversiere (Heugel LP 50).
Dittersdorf	Concerto in E minor (Möseler 54; the score is correct but the published parts are edited).
Gluck	Concerto in G major (Amadeus BP 2061).
Grétry	Concerto in C major (Noetzel-Pegasus).
Handel	Sonatas for fl., b.c. (Bärenreiter 4003, 4040; Faber).
	Sonatas for 2 violins (or fl. and vn.) and b.c., Op. 2 (Bärenreiter 4029).
Joseph Haydn	3 Trios for fl., vc., kbd. (Doblinger 512/513/514).
	3 'London' Trios for 2 fl., vc. (Peters 4972).
Michael Haydn	Concerto in D major (1766) (Editio Musica Budapest; the score is correct but the separate flute part is edited).
	Concerto in D major (a different concerto from the above) (Haydn-Mozart Presse).
Hotteterre	Suite in E minor, fl. and b.c. (Bärenreiter 3316).
Hummel	Sonata in G major, Op. 2 No. 2 (Doblinger 181).
	Sonata in D major, Op. 50 (Doblinger 148; Heinrichshofen 6124).

	Sonata in A major, Op. 64 (Doblinger 473).
W. A. Mozart	Concerto in C major for fl., hp., K. 299 (Bärenreiter).
	Concerto in G major, K. 313 (Amadeus BP 2693; Bärenreiter 6817, which also contains the Andante in C, K. 315; Novello).
	Concerto in D major, K. 314 (Amadeus BP 2694; Bärenreiter 6818; Novello, which also contains the Andante, K. 315).
	Andante in C major, K. 315 (Amadeus BP 519; Bärenreiter; Novello).
	4 Quartets for fl., vn., va., vc., K. 285, 285a, 285b, 298 (Bärenreiter 4405).
	6 Sonatas, K. 10–15 (Bärenreiter 4756).
	Sonata in G major, K. 301 (Bärenreiter 4774 for vn. version; Voggenreiter for fl. reconstruction by Ricarda and Knut Bröhl).
F. Philidor	Pièces pour la flûte traversière (Schott ED 12205/6).
N. Piccinni	Concerto in D major (Doblinger 807).
Rameau	Pièces de Clavecin en concerts for hpd., fl./vn., gamba/vn. (Bärenreiter 3803).
Ries	Sonata in E flat major, Op. 169 (Bärenreiter 19107; Musica Rara).
Schubert	Variations, Op. 160 (Bärenreiter 6819 and Schott Universal UT 50087 both include the first version of Variation V; Breitkopf 6658; Peters 156c).
Telemann	12 Fantasias for fl. unacc. (Musica Rara 2167 includes a facsimile of the original print; Bärenreiter 2971 and Peters 9715 contain some divergences from the original).
	Sonatas for 2 fl., Op. 2 (Bärenreiter 2979/80; 12 additional sonatas are in Bärenreiter 2975/76 and 2977/78).
	12 'Methodical' Sonatas (Bärenreiter 2951).
	Concerto in E minor for fl., rec. (Bärenreiter HM 124).
	Musique de Table (*Tafelmusik*):
	Solo in B minor for fl., b.c. (Bärenreiter 3537)
	Trio in E minor for fl., ob., b.c. (Bärenreiter 3541)
	Quartet in G major for fl., ob., vn., b.c. (Bärenreiter 3534)
	Quartet in D minor for 2 fl., rec., b.c. (Bärenreiter 3539).
Vivaldi	6 Concertos, Op. 10 (Ricordi).
Weber	Trio in G minor, Op. 63 for fl., vc., pf. (Eulenburg).

IO

Bringing It All to Life: Advice to the Contemporary Player

THE flute treatises from the eighteenth and nineteenth centuries contain sufficient instruction to enable the old instrument to be played well by contemporary players without requiring a comparative knowledge of the modern flute. However, many modern traverso-players have come to the instrument from the Boehm flute, and many will continue to do so. Comparisons between the two types of flutes can be helpful. Such basic musical concepts as tone, pitch, intonation, tuning and temperament, acoustics, articulation, vibrato, tempo, and notation should be reconsidered by the modern player when preparing to learn the traverso because these concepts may have somewhat different meanings to the modern player from those they had to flautists in previous centuries.

Tone

Modern Boehm flute-players who take up the traverso should be prepared to produce sounds quite different from those of the metal Boehm flute. There are a number of factors regarding the traverso which cause this to happen: its embouchure hole and tone holes are smaller than those of the Boehm flute; its bore is conical rather than cylindrical; it is made of wood or ivory rather than metal.

While we can never know what flautists of the baroque and classical eras really sounded like, we can read contemporary descriptions of the sound. Quantz (1752) described his ideal flute sound as 'that which more nearly resembles a contralto than a soprano, or which imitates the chest tones of the human voice ... a clear, penetrating, thick, round, masculine and withal pleasant sound'.[1] Antoine Mahaut (1759) wrote that 'the embouchure is correct

---

[1] J. J. Quantz, *On Playing the Flute*, ed. and trans. Edward R. Reilly (London: Faber & Faber, 1966; 2nd edn., 1985), 50.

when the tone is full, round and clear. It is beautiful when, in addition, the tone is soft, delicate, resonant and graceful.[2] In 1791 Tromlitz wrote,

Because not all persons are fond of the same kind of tone, but differ amongst themselves in this matter . . . it is therefore impossible to establish a tone-quality that can be recognised as beautiful in general. If the tone is clear, resonant and pleasing, it will indeed please the majority, but there will certainly be some who find something to censure about it here and there. This goes to show that tone is a matter of taste . . . I say, the only model on which an instrumentalist should form his tone is a beautiful human voice; and as far as I am concerned a human voice that is beautiful is one that is bright, full and resonant, of masculine strength, but not shrieking; soft, but not hollow; in short, for me a beautiful voice is full of timbre, rounded, singing, soft and flexible.[3]

Tromlitz also wrote that 'a great deal also depends on the instrument. A bad instrument cannot produce a good tone.'[4]

Pitch

Playing music at historic pitches is not simply an academic exercise. On the contrary, it enables our period instruments to be played at the pitch for which they were originally designed. Different pitches give us different feelings about the music we play, and this ultimately affects our interpretations.

Players of modern instruments generally think in terms of one standard pitch, usually A=440, although some ensembles now play at A=442 or A=444. Modern instruments are designed to play at one or the other of these standardized pitches, and the player doesn't need to give further thought to pitch except to play 'in tune' at the given pitch of the instrument.

Players of baroque and classical instruments have a different challenge, because pitch was anything but standardized in the baroque and classical eras.[5] By a kind of unwritten current international consensus among professional early music players, French baroque pitch is now A=392 (about a whole tone below modern pitch); the German-born baroque composers are played at A=415 (about a half-step below modern pitch), and classical music is performed at A=430. Clearly, these selected pitches are a compromise of convenience.[6]

---

[2] Antoine Mahaut, *A New Method for Learning to Play the Transverse Flute*, trans. and ed. Eileen Hadidian (Bloomington, Ind.: Indiana University Press, 1989), 5.

[3] Johann George Tromlitz, *The Virtuoso Flute-Player*, trans. and ed. Ardal Powell (Cambridge: Cambridge University Press, 1991), ch. 6, para. 2.

[4] Ibid. para. 1.

[5] A discerning exposition of the research which has been done in recent years regarding pitches in use in Bach's day is found in Bruce Haynes, 'Johann Sebastian Bach's Pitch Standards: The Woodwind Perspective', *Journal of the American Musical Instrument Society*, 11 (1985).

[6] See Bruce Haynes, 'Generic 415', *Traverso*, 1: 4 (1989).

Historically, the range of pitches used in the past was wider than stated here. Modern players of period instruments must learn to choose a performing pitch which faithfully represents the pitch of the music from a given era and to choose an appropriate instrument which sounds good at that pitch. If one plays Bach at a classical pitch of A=430 or higher, a certain warmth and darkness to the sound will be lost. Likewise, if one plays Haydn or Mozart at a baroque pitch of A=415, some of the characteristic lightness and brightness will be lost. Of course, the design of the instrument and how it is played are also factors which contribute to the character of a performance. It is not wrong to play Mozart at A=415 or Bach at A=430; however, sonoroties are thus created which are subtly different from the ideal which would best serve the music.

The different pitches from the different eras also present problems in planning the musical content of a programme for modern audiences. What does one do regarding pitch if a programme contains both French baroque and German baroque music, or both baroque and classical compositions? There is no formula answer for this. Perhaps one can play an all-baroque first half and an all-classical second half, taking time during the interval to put in a shorter centre piece on the traverso and to allow string-players (if any) to tune up to the higher pitch. In general, string-players should not be expected to crank up the pitch in a short minute or two, because their instruments will not hold the new tuning very well.

Intonation

Good intonation is essential to a good musical performance. Modern metal flutes are not only well tuned; their pitch is also reasonably stable. Such is not the case of the traverso. Its scale contains 'problem' notes which a skilled player learns to mask. Moreover, the traverso is also subject to pitch fluctuations greater than one encounters on the modern metal flute. The wood or ivory from which the traverso is made respond more noticeably to changes in temperature and humidity than does metal. Players of period instruments should develop an especially acute ear for good intonation. Heavy or continuous vibrato, which disguises the true pitch of a note, is unidiomatic on the traverso and should not be used to cover up intonational deficiencies.

Tuning and Temperament

In addition to listening carefully to intonation, Renaissance and baroque flute players must also learn to play in systems of tuning which are different from the equal temperament universally used by today's modern instrumentalists. The original surviving flutes from the Renaissance and baroque eras do not play in equal temperament, nor should modern replicas based upon them.

The history of tuning and temperament is very complex and cannot be covered even in summary in a book as concise as this one.[7] The modern piano is tuned to equal temperament, which divides the octave into twelve equal semitones. The interval of a third is tuned wider than a pure third. If the thirds were pure, three major thirds played in succession would not quite reach an octave, being short by a small interval called a lesser diesis. Temperament on an instrument with set tuning, such as a keyboard, is concerned with reconciling this problem. One should be familiar with the theories of historical systems of tuning and should be able to hear the different effects which various systems of tuning have upon music. It is a special experience to play in unequal temperaments. The tonal structure of a piece of music is heightened; the more remote keys sound more pungent.

There are two aspects of temperament which are of importance to the traverso player, one being the inherent tuning of the traverso, the other the tuning of the accompanying instruments, such as a harpsichord. If a replica traverso is true to its historically correct tuning, then one could ask for nothing more. It is a temptation for modern makers of replicas to lean towards equal temperament, which many buyers seem to prefer. If buyers are indifferent to historic temperaments, so will the makers be. Serious makers and players should attempt to replicate the approximate temperament which was original to the specific flute, or at least to the time and place of the instrument. Of course Renaissance and baroque flutes have always had their peculiar internal tuning problems, and the intervening centuries may have changed the tuning of any given surviving instrument by the shrinking of the interior bore. However, by studying many flutes by one maker, or flutes by different makers active in the same time and place, it should be possible for a modern maker to arrive at a general idea about temperament of a specific instrument.

Renaissance flutes in replica should be designed to play in mean-tone tuning, which was in general use at the time that Renaissance flutes were played. Essentially what this means in practical terms for today's player is that major thirds are pure, smaller than in equal temperament. A player must hear and play a lower E, B, F♯, C♯, G♯, a higher B♭ and E♭. Moreover, E♭ must be played higher than D♯, and A♭ must be higher than G♯. Mean-tone tuning was more or less forgotten in the nineteenth century and has made a come-back only relatively recently, a result of the studies of historical tuning and temperament which have been made as a critical part of the early music revival.

---

[7] An excellent summary is the article on temperament by Mark Lindley in the *New Grove Dictionary of Music and Musicians*, repr. in the *New Grove Dictionary of Musical Instruments*.

Regarding the other aspect of tuning (relative to the accompanying set-tuned instrument such as lute, theorbo, or harpsichord), the traverso player should not naïvely accept whatever tuning is offered but should have a voice in choosing the temperament. Of course, fretted instruments such as the lute have tuning problems different from those of harpsichords; nevertheless, a temperament should be chosen which is compatible with the temperament of the traverso.

The tuning identified as 'Werckmeister 3', for example, is a satisfactory tuning for a harpsichord intended to perform with the baroque flute, as is the tuning system of Francisco Antonio Vollotti, a Paduan organist who worked in the mid-eighteenth century. Another tuning which accommodates the special peculiarities of the traverso is Lionel Party's modified version of *tempérament ordinaire*, a French tuning used at the end of the seventeenth century. A well-known harpsichordist and teacher at the Juilliard School in New York and the Curtis Institute of Music in Philadelphia, Mr Party has set forth the following steps for tuning a harpsichord to this irregular temperament.

1. Start with A415(a′).
2. Copy a′ with a (octave lower)
3. Tune d′ a fifth from a′. Make d′ as high as possible to get a very small albeit usable and tolerable fifth. How small it can be made depends on taste and also on the properties of the individual harpsichord.
4. Tune e′ a fifth from a. Make this fifth as small as d′–a′.
5. Tune b′ a fifth from e′. Make this fifth as small as the previous two.
6. Tune b a perfect octave from b′.
7. Tune f♯′ a fifth from b. Make this fifth small but not as small as the previous three.
8. Check triad d′-f♯′-a′ (tune f♯″ from f♯′ and try it with the flute's. It should be in tune. If it is not in tune with the flute's, adjust all the fifths already tuned accordingly).
9. Tune c♯″ a perfect, with no beats, fifth from f♯′.
10. Tune c♯′ a perfect octave from c♯″.
11. Tune g♯′ a fifth from c♯′. Depending on the size of the previous fifths, this fifth should be made either perfect or bigger than perfect.
12. Go back to d′ (step 3).Tune d″ a perfect octave from d′.
13. Tune g′ to d″. Make this fifth as small as possible. Check triad g′-b′-d″. The major third should be very small but not perfect, with no beats.
14. Tune c′ a fifth from g′. Make this fifth as small as possible. Check triad c′-e′-g′. The major third should be very small but not perfect.

15. Tune c″ a perfect octave from c′.
16. Tune f′ a fifth from c″. Make this fifth small but not as small as the previous one. Check triad f′-a′-c″. The major third should be good but not as small as c′-e′.
17. Tune b♭ a perfect, with no beats, fifth from f′.
18. Tune b♭′ a perfect octave from b♭.
19. The last note to be tuned is e♭′ (d♯′).
20. Tune e♭″ a perfect octave from e♭′. These two notes should make fifths of equal size with g♯′ (a♭′) and b♭′ (a♯′). These two fifths should be perfect or bigger than perfect depending on the size of the other ten fifths.
21. Then tune the remainder of the harpsichord by tuning octaves.

The advantage of this tuning system is that it is easy to move one note here or there to adjust for the special requirements of the traverso (or whatever wind instrument is involved).

Electronic tuning devices capable of giving historic temperaments are rapidly coming into use. One highly versatile tuner is the battery-operated Poletti tuner DTS-2D. This small device gives any pitch standard that is useful or historically valid and offers forty-two temperaments, including nineteen versions of meantone temperament, Werckmeister 3 and 4, Vollotti-1/6, and equal temperament.[8]

In playing unaccompanied music on the traverso or in ensemble with string instruments where temperament is established by the spontaneous tuning of each note as it is played, one need not be so concerned about what temperament one is playing. Your ear, and the ears of your colleagues, should tell you what is acceptable and what is not.

The traverso first became an instrument capable of playing in equal temperament when it evolved into a four-keyed instrument with the new keys for F, G♯, and B♭. Crucially important in achieving this equal temperament is utilizing the correct fingering for f♯′ and f♯″ on the four-keyed instrument. The f♯′ and f♯″ had always been so comparatively low in pitch that it had effectively prevented the traverso from being equally tempered. With the invention of the F key, the pitch of f♯′ (and f♯″) was able to be raised by opening the additional vent provided by the F key as part of the regular f♯ fingering and, for the first time, the traverso could be played in equal temperament. The four-keyed flute evolved at just about the time that lowered leading tones in music were being replaced by the new fashion of higher leading tones. It is also interesting to note that the four-keyed flute can be played as if it were an unequally tempered one-keyed flute simply by ignoring the three new keys.

[8] The Poletti tuner is available from the Harpsichord Centre, 2751 West Broadway, Eagle Rock, Los Angeles, CA 90041, USA.

Acoustics and Hall Size

Since the early nineteenth century, the flute has been designed to be played as a concert-hall instrument, capable of being heard in auditoriums accommodating thousands of people and maintaining its presence in the ever-expanding symphony orchestra. Such was not the case with the Renaissance, baroque, and classical flutes, however. They were generally played in churches, palace rooms, and small concert rooms. During the modern revival of these instruments, it is desirable that they should continue to be played in rooms of a size comparable to those for which they were originally made. The Hanover Square Rooms in London, where the Bach–Abel and Haydn–Salomon concerts were held during the last quarter of the eighteenth century, measured about 24 m. (79 feet) by 9.75 m. (32 feet). The Concert spirituel was given for most of the eighteenth century in the Tuileries' Salle des Cent Suisse the dimensions of which were about 18 m. (59 feet) by 16 m. (52.5 feet).[9] To play a traverso in a large modern concert hall is to do a disservice to the instrument and to early music. Much of the essence of the traverso is to be found in the subtlety of its nuances, the refinement of the details, and the patterns of the varied articulations. When these aspects of the traverso are lost in the vast spaces of a large auditorium, we are also losing the fundamental characteristics of the instrument as well as the communicative powers of the music. Attempts to force the sound or to project the tone usually have negative results. The instrument must be allowed to speak on its own terms. It should be played in settings where audiences are able to respond to its most refined aspects. If one must play in a large concert hall, discreet amplification may be the best solution, as Stephen Preston suggests. If there is a choice of a performance venue, churches or large rooms rather than concert halls should be given serious consideration. Moreover, the acoustics should be somewhat reverberant, not dry as are most modern concert halls, because reverberant acoustics tend to flatter the traverso.

Articulation

Standard articulation on the metal Boehm-system flute is a rather straightforward matter. Henri Altès (1826–99) gives five different types of articulation.[10] Single tonguing requires a *tu* syllable; mezzo-staccato tonguing is done with *du*. When the speed of the music becomes too fast for single tonguing,

---

[9] For additional information about proportions of 18th-cent. concert rooms, see Neal Zaslaw, 'Toward the Revival of the Classical Orchestra', *Proceedings of the Royal Musical Association*, 103, (1976–7), 166–7.
[10] See H. Altès, *Célèbre Méthode Complète de Flûte* (Paris: Alphonse Leduc, 1956), 212.

double tonguing is employed, using *tu-ku* syllables. Triple tonguing is *tu-ku-tu*. Dotted rhythms are tongued using compound strokes of the tongue, either T-D for duple rhythm or T-TD for triple rhythm.

The very dulcet nature of the tone of the traverso requires more varied and interesting articulations in order to give it presence and character. Practitioners of early music should ever be conscious of the rhetorical origins of music. Syllables as part of articulation play an important and creative part of playing the traverso. No two performers will necessarily agree upon which syllables to use throughout a piece. Patterns of articulation are analogous to patterns of speech. Using the same articulation on a succession of notes is less desirable than varying it, perhaps using pairs of syllables, alternating *tu* with *ru* (Hotteterre) or *ti* with *ri* (Quantz). Quantz also advocated an articulation based on the syllables *did'll*. For articulations involving slurred groups of notes, it is not enough simply to re-articulate the next note after a slur. There should be a lift at the end of the slur, a lift being a brief instant of silence following the release of the sound. The result is a lightness not readily achieved on the modern metal flute. The importance of articulation to such authorities as Hotteterre, Quantz, and, above all, Tromlitz is self-evident in the comparative length and detail of the chapters on articulation in their respective treatises. Equally revealing are Quantz's instructions regarding articulation which appear throughout the book known as *Solfeggi*, already discussed in Chapters 8 and 9.

Vibrato

Vibrato on the modern flute is used lavishly, in many cases virtually continuously, by contemporary players. It is regarded as essential for giving the flute the brilliance and projection needed for it to be heard in our modern symphony orchestras and in our stadium-sized concert halls. A tone without vibrato is considered to be lifeless and dull.

Although there was undoubtedly a great deal of variation in the amount and use of vibrato by different players on the traverso in the baroque and classical ages, the taste of the time obliged performers to regard vibrato as an ornament. It was generally used only on longer notes as an expressive device, certainly not continuously. Continuous vibrato reduces the opportunity to be expressive in other ways, such as shaping minute gradations of dynamics. Sometimes the use of vibrato was notated in printed music by a wavy line, as may be seen in Fig. 35, the Allemande of Pierre Danican Philidor's *Huitième Suitte* from his *Deuxième Œuvre*, 1718.

Modern vibrato is usually produced by a pulsation of the wind stream controlled by muscles in the throat and the diaphragm. Vibrato on the traverso

FIG. 35. Allemande from *Huitième Suitte* (*Deuxième Œuvre*), by Pierre Danican
Philidor (Paris, 1718)

is not usually made in this manner. Instead, the player's finger fluctuates at the
edge of an open finger-hole on the instrument or sometimes opening and
closing an entire hole. The French call this vibration *flattement*, a name which
reminds us that the effect actually involves flattening a given note and then
returning it to the correct pitch in a fast fluctuation. Not until De Lusse's
treatise of about 1760 was vibrato referred to as involving the pulsation of the
wind stream, blowing the syllables, *hou, hou, hou*, and doing it as often as
possible.

It is currently fashionable for some of the leading traverso players to play
without any vibrato. A performer such as Barthold Kuijken plays with such
great art that one does not notice the absence of vibration in his tone. Other
players may limit vibrato to the use of *flattement*, while still others may use
occasional discreet pulsations in the wind stream. These are personal decisions

involving taste and aesthetics. The great Swiss baroque oboist and recorder-player, Michel Piguet, when asked if he played his instruments without vibrato, responded by saying, 'I don't play without anything.'

Tempo

Players of early music on period instruments have discovered that appropriate historical styles and techniques encourage us to consider new ideas about old tempos. The transparency of the baroque or classical orchestra, the lightness of the bow on the strings, the absence of throbbing vibrato, the sparkle of a harpsichord continuo—all contribute to a different sonority and, hence, to a reconsideration of tempos. Since many movements in baroque and classical music are based upon the dance, a knowledge of dance rhythms and steps contemporary with the music will aid players in finding appropriate tempos for those movements. Quantz's indications of tempos, as given in his treatise, should be applied to performances of mid-eighteenth-century German music on period instruments.[11]

Of specific interest to baroque flautists are the ornamented slow movements of the Bach sonatas. If one strips away the embellishments and plays the melody in a theoretically simplified version, one should find a viable tempo. Then, in restoring Bach's original ornamentation, one should keep the same tempo. It will almost always be faster than traditional modern flute interpretations. Another revelation regarding tempo in Bach concerns the Ouverture of the B minor Suite for traverso and strings. The Australian organist and musicologist, John O'Donnell, has convincingly demonstrated that the historically correct tempo for this Ouverture is $\downarrow$ = 50–56, about twice the speed of 'traditional' intepretations of this work.[12]

Technical considerations of the traverso, on the other hand, will sometimes result in slower tempos than those which the modern flute can handle. Most modern players take the Badinerie of Bach's B minor Suite at breakneck speed. Bach's flute-player might have taken it at a somewhat slower tempo to accommodate the technical realities of the one-keyed flute.

Notation

Except for some of the post-war avant-garde music, traditional modern notation is extremely explicit. Virtually nothing is left to the discretion of the performer.

---

[11] See Quantz, *On Playing the Flute*, 283–92.
[12] See John O'Donnell, 'The French Style and the Overtures of Bach', *Early Music*, 7: 2 (1979), 190–6.

Dynamics, tempos, and articulations are all spelled out in meticulous detail by the composer. The modern flautist is trained to respect and obey every mark placed on the printed page by the composer.

In the baroque and classical ages, however, composers wrote music with the expectation that performers would invent dynamics, create articulations, and add ornamentation and embellishments. Keyboard players were expected to realize the figured bass at sight, filling in the harmonies which the composer had indicated with a kind of notational shorthand. As a result, the printed page of a typical piece of baroque or classical music will usually appear to be barren except for the notes and an occasional ornament, as shown in Fig. 35. This does not mean that such music should be played in a bleak, inexpressive manner. On the contrary, it is an invitation to the performer to think creatively, to bring the music to life by whatever legitimate, tasteful musical means can be produced.

Modern flautists generally learn to read only one clef in order to play the flute: the treble clef. Traverso-players who perform French baroque music, using original editions, must also learn to read the French G clef (commonly called the French violin clef), which was used for all flute music published in France until about 1725. This clef places the music an interval of a third lower on the staff, so that the top line is a″. An easy way to read this clef is to imagine one is reading the bass clef and then transpose it two octaves higher. (Far better, of course, is to learn to read the French G clef properly.)

Assembling the Traverso

In assembling the modern flute, the embouchure hole is usually rotated to be in a straight line with the centre of the principal keys. Most players agree that this gives the ideal relative position of the keys to enable the fingers to reach the keys in the most natural, relaxed manner.[13] This positioning does not apply to the baroque or classical flute. Quantz suggests lining up the outer edge of the embouchure hole with the inner edge of the finger-holes.[14] In other words, the head piece should be rolled in towards the player the equivalent of the diameter of the embouchure hole.[15] Many flautists who play both the Boehm-system

---

[13] Walfrid Kujala, a member of the Chicago Symphony Orchestra, recommends rotating the head piece of the modern flute so that the outer edge of the embouchure hole is lined up with the key mechanism. See Kujala, *The Flutist's Progress* (Winnetka, Ill.: Progress Press, 1970), 20.

[14] Quantz, *On Playing the Flute*, 36.

[15] François Devienne, writing in 1795, stated also that an embouchure hole which is aligned with the finger-holes forces the player to lift the elbow too high or to lower the head. He recommnds rotating the head piece in such a way that the hole is inside a line with the other finger-holes, similar to the advice rendered by Quantz. See Devienne, *Nouvelle Méthode, Théorique et Pratique Pour La Flute* (Paris: Imbault,

flute and the flauto traverso find no conflict in setting the embouchure hole differently for each type of instrument.

Fingers and Fingering

On the modern flute, we are taught to hold our fingers as close to the key cups as possible. This is the smoothest, most efficient way to play. This advice does not apply to the traverso, however. If the fingers are held too close to the finger-holes, the pitch of the note being played may be accidentally flattened. This does not occur on the Boehm flute because the venting of the hole occurs between the key's pad and the tone hole rim.

The multi-keyed classical flute is a closed G♯ instrument. Anyone who plays the Boehm-system flute with open G♯ key will have major problems in taking up the multi-keyed simple-system instrument.[16]

There is a wide variety of fingering options available to players of the traverso irrespective of the number of keys on the instrument—more than on the Boehm-system flute if one excludes the avant-garde fingerings for microtones, multiphonics, and for producing varied tone colours. Each traverso is different, the instrument being considerably less standardized than modern Boehm-system metal flutes. The traverso-player must therefore be prepared to use fingerings other than standard ones if the instrument being played should require it.

Avoiding Mixing Modern and Period Instruments

The traverso should ideally be played only with other period instruments, and preferably with players who have studied the appropriate styles. Differences in temperament, pitch, timbre, and volume of sound place period and modern instruments in different worlds. It is difficult enough for the sweet-sounding traverso to hold its own in an ensemble of period instruments; it becomes almost completely lost in the company of modern instruments. Moreover, the

---

*c.*1794); facsimile edn. (Florence: Studio per Edizioni Scelte, 1984), 5. Many flute-makers aligned their maker's mark on all pieces in such a way as to indicate their preferred degree of rotation of the head piece. From the location of the maker's mark on to the foot piece, it is also possible to ascertain if antique one-keyed flutes were intended to be played left-handed.

[16] One possible solution to this problem might be to redesign the G♯ key on the simple-system flute, changing it from closed to open. Or the key might be completely removed, exposing the G♯ hole, which can then be covered directly by the little finger of the left hand. The instrument could then be played as an open G♯ instrument.

gentle, unforced manner of playing the traverso is no match for the intense, vibrant style of playing modern instruments.

For ensemble playing, if one cannot find string-players who perform on proper period instruments, it is possible to compromise by substituting baroque or classical bows for modern, replacing metal strings with gut, and lowering pitch. String-players should use less vibrato, play in low positions, and use light, lifted bow strokes as opposed to martelé. The primary expression should take place in the bow arm. This approach helps to reconcile modern string instruments with the flauto traverso.

Conductors are a creation of the modern (i.e. Romantic) symphony orchestra. In the baroque and classical eras, conductors as we know them today did not exist. In general, more responsibility rested on the individual players than is the case in the modern orchestra. The principal violin (leader) or keyboard player generally assumed the responsibility for starting and stopping a piece and for keeping time. It is much easier for string-players to take a downbeat by watching a violinist giving it with the bow on the string than by observing a conductor waving a baton. The ideal of baroque and classical performance is to play in chamber-music fashion, the players depending upon ears and eyes for good ensemble and ears alone for balance and blend.

Learning from Other Instruments

Much of what we learn about performance style from a practical standpoint may be gleaned by listening, observing, and playing with other period instruments and singers. The string-player's bow teaches us about inflection and variety. From the voice we learn about speech patterns and the sounds of vowels and consonants, each language offering a different experience. The harpsichord reveals much about ornamentation and rhythm. By listening to other wind instruments we learn about tone and articulation. Many of the questions which might be asked are frequently answered simply by trying the music. For example, problems of balance often resolve themselves with period instruments. If one has played baroque or classical music first on modern instruments, it can be an exhilarating experience to hear the effortlessly achieved proper balances which had been so problematical on modern instruments.

If one understands what the baroque violinist is doing differently from the modern counterpart, one might try the same comparative ideas on the traverso. For example, if the baroque or classical violinist eschews the 'seamless' bowing technique of the modern violinist for a lighter, more varied bowing, the traverso-player might try the equivalent change by lessening the continuous intensity of the windstream and 'lifting' at the ends of slurred groups in the overall shape of a phrase. The interplay and cross-fertilization of ideas can be richly rewarding to all who make the effort to listen, to learn, and to play on period instruments.[17]

[17] For additional reading on the interrelationship of performance on modern and baroque instruments, see Mary Louise Poor, 'Problems of Transference from Boehm to Baroque Flute', *Newsletter of the National Flute Association* 6: 3 (1981), and Christopher Krueger, 'Playing Baroque Music on the Modern Flute', *Flutist Quarterly*, 13: 1 (1988).

APPENDIX

Useful Addresses

Addresses of noted makers of historical flutes

Roderick Cameron
PO Box 438
640 School Street
Mendocino, CA 95460
USA
Summer residence and workshop:
39 Union Street,
Nairn, Scotland IV12 2PR

Folkers & Powell
R. D. 3, Box 56
Hudson NY 12534
USA

Friedrich von Huene
65 Boylston Street
Brookline, MA 02146
USA

Thomas Prescott
14 Grant Road
Lyme, NH 03768
USA

Rudolph Tutz
Maria-Theresienstrasse 8
A-6020 Innsbruck
Austria

Dr A Weemaels
108 Avenue Prince de Ligne
1180 Brussels
Belgium

Addresses of auction houses

Miss Frances Gillham
Director, Music Department
Christie, Manson & Woods Ltd.
8 King Street, St. James's
London, SW1Y 6QT
UK

Edward Stollar
Director, Musical Instruments
Phillips, Son & Neale
Blenstock House
7 Blenheim Street, New Bond Street
London, W1Y 0AS
UK

Graham Wells
Director, Musical Instruments
Sotheby's
34 & 35 New Bond Street
London W1A 2AA
UK

Addresses of dealers in antique flutes

Tony Bingham
11 Pond Street
London, NW3 2PN
UK

Peter H. Bloom
29 Newbury Street
Somerville, MA 02144
USA

Bernhard von Hünerbein
Lintgasse 22–26
D-5000 Köln 1
Germany

Fred Oster
Vintage Instruments
1529 Pine Street
Philadelphia, PA 19102
USA

David and Nina Shorey
PO Box 92
Bowdoinham, ME 04008
USA

Sweetheart Flute Co.
32 South Maple Street
Enfield, CT 06082
USA

Wichita Band Instrument Co., Inc.
2525 East Douglas
Wichita, KS 67211
USA

Wurlitzer-Bruck
60 Riverside Drive
New York, NY 10024
USA

Addresses of early music shops

The Early Music Shop
38 Manningham Lane
Bradford, West Yorkshire BD1 3EA
UK

Schott Early Music Shop
48 Great Marlborough Street
London, W1V 2BN
UK

Early Music Shop of New England
59 Boylston Street
Brookline, MA 02146
USA

BIBLIOGRAPHY

Books

AGRICOLA, MARTIN, *Musica instrumentalis deudsch* (Wittenberg: Georg Rhau, 1529); facsimile edn. (Hildesheim: Georg Olms Verlag, 1969).

—— *Musica instrumentalis deudsch* (Wittenberg: Georg Rhau, 1545); photo-repr. ed. Robert Eitner, *Publikation älterer praktischer und theoretischer Musikwerke* xxiv/20 (Leipzig: Breitkopf & Härtel, 1896).

ALEXANDER, JAMES, *Alexander's Complete Preceptor for the Flute* (London: The Author, 1821).

ALTÈS, HENRI, *Célèbre Méthode Complète de Flûte* (Paris: Alphonse Leduc, 1956).

ARBEAU, THOINOT, *Orchesographie* (Lengres: Jehan des Preyz, 1589); facsimile edn., ed. François Lesure (Geneva: Minkoff Reprint, 1972); English trans. Mary Stewart Evans, with new introduction and notes by Julia Sutton (New York: Dover Publications, 1967).

BACH, CARL PHILIPP EMANUEL, *Essay on the True Art of Playing Keyboard Instruments*, trans. and ed. William J. Mitchell (New York: W. W. Norton, 1949; London: Cassell, 1951).

BAINES, ANTHONY, *European and American Musical Instruments* (New York: The Viking Press, 1966; London: Batsford, 1966).

BATE, PHILIP, *The Flute* (London: Ernest Benn, 1969; New York: W. W. Norton, 1969, 2nd impression, 1975).

BEALE, JOHN, *A Complete Guide to the Art of Playing the German Flute* (London: Goulding, D'Almaine, & Potter, *c.*1815).

BLOOM, PETER H., *A Practical & Tuneful Method for the Baroque Flute* (Somerville, Mass.: Author, 1989).

BOEHM, THEOBALD, *The Flute and Flute-Playing*, trans. and annotated Dayton C. Miller (Cleveland, Oh.: Dayton C. Miller, 1922; repr. New York: Dover Publications, 1964).

BOYDEN, DAVID D., *The History of Violin Playing from Its Origins to 1761 and Its Relationship to the Violin and Violin Music* (London: Oxford University Press, 1965).

BROWN, HOWARD MAYER, *Embellishing Sixteenth-Century Music* (London: Oxford University Press, 1976).

BROWN, MAURICE J. E., *Schubert's Variations* (London: Macmillan, 1954).

CAMBINI, J. M., *Methode pour la Flûte traversiere* (Paris: Gaveaux, *c.* 1796–7; facsimile edn. (Florence: Studio per Edizioni Scelte, 1984).

CORRETTE, MICHEL, *Methode pour apprendre aisément à joüer de la Flute traversiere* (Paris: Boivin, *c.*1740); facsimile edns. (Hildesheim: Georg Olms Verlag, 1975; Buren: Frits Knuf, 1978); English trans. Carol Reglin Farrar, *Method for Easily Learning to Play on the Transverse Flute* (Brooklyn: Institute of Medieval Music, 1970).

148   *Bibliography*

DART, THURSTON, *The Interpretation of Music* (London: Hutchinson's University
     Library, 1954).
DE LUSSE, [CHARLES], *L'Art de la flûte traversiere* (Paris: Addresses Ordinaires de
     Musique, c.1760); facsimile edns. (Buren: Frits Knuf, 1980; Geneva: Minkoff, 1973;
     Columbus, Oh.: Early Music Facsimiles, n.d.).
DEVIENNE, FRANÇOIS, *Célèbre Méthode Complète de Flûte* (Paris: Alphonse Leduc, 1909).
—— *Nouvelle Méthode Théorique et Pratique Pour La Flute* (Paris: Imbault, c.1794);
     facsimile edns. (Florence: Studio per Edizioni Scelte, 1984; Buren, Frits Knuf,
     forthcoming).
DOLMETSCH, ARNOLD, *The Interpretation of the Music of the XVIIth and XVIIIth Centuries
     Revealed by Contemporary Evidence* (London: Novello, 1915; rev. edn., 1946; repr.,
     Seattle: University of Washington Press, 1969).
DONINGTON, ROBERT, *A Performer's Guide to Baroque Music* (London: Faber & Faber,
     1973).
—— *Baroque Music: Style and Performance* (London: Faber Music, 1982).
—— *The Interpretation of Early Music* (new version, London: Faber & Faber, 1974; New
     York: St Martin's Press, 1974).
EYCK, JACOB VAN, *Der Fluyten Lust-hof* (Amsterdam: Paulus Matthysz, 1646); facsimile
     edn., ed. Kees Otten (Amsterdam, B. V. Muziekhandel Saul B. Groen, n.d.).
FULLER, DAVID, *Mechanical Musical Instruments as a Source for the Study of Notes Inégales*
     (Cleveland Heights, Oh.: Divisions, 1979).
GEMINIANI, FRANCESCO, *The Art of Playing on the Violin*, facsimile edn., ed. David
     Boyden (London: Oxford University Press, 1952).
GIANNINI, TULA, *Great Flute Makers of France: The Lot and Godfroy Families,
     1650–1900* (London: Tony Bingham, 1993).
GILLIAM, LAURA E., and LICHTENWANGER, WILLIAM, *The Dayton C. Miller Flute
     Collection: A Checklist of the Instruments* (Washington, DC: Library of Congress, 1961).
GRANOM, LEWIS, *Plain and Easy Instructions for Playing on the German-Flute*, (London:
     T. Bennett, 1766).
GUNN, JOHN, *The Art of Playing the German-Flute* (London: The Author, c.1793);
     facsimile edn. (Marion, Ia.: Janice Dockendorff Boland, n.d.).
HARTIG, LINDA BISHOP, *Johann George Tromlitz's 'Unterricht die Flöte zu Spielen': A
     Translation and Comparative Study* (Ann Arbor, Mich.: University Microfilms Inter-
     national, 1982).
HASKELL, HARRY, *The Early Music Revival: A History* (London: Thames & Hudson,
     1988).
HELM, E. EUGENE, *Thematic Catalogue of the Works of Carl Philipp Emanuel Bach* (New
     Haven, Conn.: Yale University Press, 1989).
HERON, LUKE, *A Treatise on the German Flute* (London: W. Griffin, 1771); facsimile
     edn. (Buren: Frits Knuf, 1973).
Historic Flutes from Private Collections, exhibition catalogue (New York: Metropolitan
     Museum of Art, July–Aug. 1986).
HOTTETERRE, JACQUES (LE ROMAIN), *L'Art de Preluder sur la Flûte Traversiere, sur la*

Flûte a bec, sur le Haubois, et autres Instrumens de Dessus, Op. VII (Paris: L'Auteur, 1719); facsimile edn. (Geneva: Minkoff, 1978); modern edn. (Paris: Éditions Zurfluh, 1966).

—— *Principes de la flute traversiere, ou flute d'Allemagne, de la flute a bec, ou flute douce, et du haut-bois* (Paris: Christophe Ballard, 1707; Amsterdam: Estienne Roger, 1708); facsimile edn. of the Roger edn. (Kassel: Bärenreiter, 1973); English trans. by David Lasocki as *Principles of the Flute, Recorder & Oboe* (London: Barrie & Rockliff/The Cresset Press, 1968); English trans. by Paul Marshall Douglas as *Rudiments of the Flute, Recorder and Oboe* (New York: Dover Publications, 1968).

HUBBARD, FRANK, *Three Centuries of Harpsichord Making* (Cambridge, Mass.: Harvard University Press, 1965).

HUGOT, ANTOINE, and WUNDERLICH, JOHANN GEORG, *Methode de Flute* (Paris: Conservatoire de Musique, 1804); facsimile edn. (Buren: Frits Knuf, 1975).

Italienische Diminutionen, ed. Richard Erig and Veronika Gutmann (Zurich, 1979; Prattica Musicale 1).

JAMBE DE FER, PHILIBERT, *L'Epitome musical* (Lyons: Michel du Bois, 1556); facsimile edn., ed. François Lesure, *Annales musicologiques*, 6 (1958–63), 341–86.

JOURNOT, NICOLE *La Flûte traversière renaissance* (thesis, Centre de Musique Ancienne, Geneva, 1985).

KEITH, ROBERT WILLIAM, *A New and Complete Preceptor for the German Flute* (London: The Author, *c.*1816–22).

KRELL, JOHN, *Kincaidiana* (Culver City, Calif.: Trio Associates, 1973).

KUJALA, WALFRID, *The Flutist's Progress* (Winnetka, Ill.: Progress Press, 1970).

LANDON, H. C. ROBBINS, *Haydn in England 1791–1794* (Bloomington, Ind.: Indiana University Press, 1976).

LASOCKI, DAVID, and MATHER, BETTY BANG, *The Classical Woodwind Cadenza* (New York: McGinnis & Marx, 1978).

LORENZO, LEONARDO DE, *My Complete Story of the Flute* (New York: The Citadel Press, 1951; repr.,Lubbock, Tex.: Texas Tech University Press, forthcoming).

MAHAUT, ANTOINE, *A New Method for Learning to Play the Transverse Flute*, English trans. Eileen Hadidian (Bloomington, Ind.: Indiana University Press, 1989).

MARSHALL, ROBERT L., *The Music of Johann Sebastian Bach: The Sources, the Style, the Significance* (New York: Schirmer Books, 1989).

MATHER, BETTY BANG, *Interpretation of French Music from 1675 to 1775 for Woodwind and Other Performers* (New York: McGinnis & Marx, 1973).

—— with KARNS, DEAN M., *Dance Rhythms of the French Baroque: A Handbook for Performance* (Indianapolis: Indiana University Press, 1987).

—— and LASOCKI, DAVID, *Free Ornamentation in Woodwind Music 1700–1775* (New York: McGinnis & Marx, 1976).

—— and—— *The Art of Preluding 1700–1830 for Flutists, Oboists, Clarinettists, and Other Performers* (New York: McGinnis & Marx, 1984).

MERSENNE, MARIN, *Harmonie universelle* (Paris: Sebastien Cramoisy, 1636); facsimile edn., ed. François Lesure (Paris: Éditions du Centre National de la Recherche

Scientifique, 1963); English trans. Roger E. Chapman (The Hague: Martinus Nijhoff, 1957).

MEYLAN, RAYMOND, *La Flûte* (Lausanne: Éditions Payot, 1974); English trans. Alfred Clayton (Portland, Ore.: Amadeus Press, 1988).

MILLER, DAYTON C., *Catalogue of Books and Literary Material Relating to the Flute and Other Musical Instruments* (Cleveland, Oh.: privately printed, 1935).

MONTAGU, JEREMY, *The Flute* (Princes Risborough: Shire Publications, 1990).

MONZANI, TEBALDO, *Instructions for the German Flute* (London: Monzani & Cimador, 1801; 2nd edn. *c.*1807).

MOZART, LEOPOLD, *A Treatise on the Fundamental Principles of Violin Playing*, trans. Editha Knocker (London: Oxford University Press, 1948; 2nd edn., 1951).

MUNROW, DAVID, *Instruments of the Middle Ages and Renaissance* (London: Oxford University Press, 1976).

NETTL, PAUL, *Forgotten Musicians* (New York: Philosophical Library, 1951).

NEUHAUS, MARGARET, *The Baroque Flute Fingering Book* (Naperville, Ill.: Flute Studio Press, 1986).

NEUMANN, FREDERICK, *Ornamentation and Improvisation in Mozart* (Princeton, NJ: Princeton University Press, 1986).

—— *Ornamentation in Baroque and Post-Baroque Music: With Special Emphasis on J. S. Bach* (Princeton, NJ: Princeton University Press, 1978).

The New Grove Dictionary of Music and Musicians, ed. Stanley Sadie, 20 vols. (London: Macmillan, 1980).

The New Grove Dictionary of Musical Instruments ed. Stanley Sadie, 3 vols. (London: Macmillan, 1984).

The New Harvard Dictionary of Music, ed. Don Randel (Cambridge, Mass.: The Belknap Press of Harvard University Press, 1986).

The New Oxford Companion to Music, ed. Denis Arnold (Oxford: Oxford University Press, 1983).

NICHOLSON, CHARLES, *Complete Preceptor for the German Flute* (London: Preston, 1816).

—— *Preceptive Lessons for the Flute* (New York: Firth & Hall, 1832–47).

O'KELLY, EVE, *The Recorder Today* (Cambridge: Cambridge University Press, 1990).

PHILLIPS, ELIZABETH V., and JACKSON, JOHN-PAUL CHRISTOPHER, *Performing Medieval and Renaissance Music: An Introductory Guide* (New York: Schirmer Books, 1986).

PRAETORIUS, MICHAEL, *Syntagma musicum* (Wolfenbüttel: Elias Holwein, 1619); facsimile edn. (Kassel: Bärenreiter, 1958); trans. of vol. ii as *Syntagma Musicum II: Organographia Parts I and II*, trans. and ed. David Z. Crookes (Oxford: Clarendon Press, 1986; Oxford Early Music Series, 7).

PRELLEUR, PETER, *The Newest Method for Learners on the German Flute*, from The Modern Musick-Master or The Universal Musician, 1731 (facsimile edn., Kassel: Bärenreiter, 1965).

PROD-HOMME, J.-G., *Écrits de Musiciens* (Paris: Mercure de France, 1912).

QUANTZ, JOHANN JOACHIM, *Versuch einer Anweisung die Flöte traversiere zu spielen* (Berlin: Johann Friedrich Voss, 1752); English trans. as *On Playing the Flute*, ed. and trans.

Edward R. Reilly (London: Faber & Faber, 1966; New York: Free Press, 1966; 2nd edn., London: Faber & Faber, 1985; New York: Schirmer books, 1985).

REEDE, RIEN DE, ed., *Concerning the Flute*, Festschrift in honour of Frans Vester (Amsterdam: Broekmans & Van Poppel, 1984).

REILLY, EDWARD R., *Quantz and His Versuch: Three Studies* (New York: American Musicological Society, distributed by Galaxy Music Corporation, 1971).

RIBOCK, JUSTUS JOHANNES HEINRICH, *Bermerkungen über die Flöte* (Stendal: bey Dan. Christ. Franzen und Grosse, 1782); facsimile edn. (Buren: Frits Knuf, 1980).

ROCKSTRO, RICHARD SHEPHERD, *The Flute* (London: Rudall & Carte, 1890; 2nd edn., 1928; repr., London: Musica Rara, 1967).

ROSEN, CHARLES, *The Classical Style* (New York: W. W. Norton, 1971; 2nd edn., 1972).

RYOM, PETER, *Répertoire des Œuvres d'Antonio Vivaldi* (Copenhagen: Engstrom & Sodring, 1986).

SCHWEDLER, MAXIMILIAN, *Des Flötenspielers erster Lehrmeister* (Heilbronn: C. F. Schmidt, 1899).

SEYFRIT, MICHAEL, *Musical Instruments in the Dayton C. Miller Collection at the Library of Congress: A Catalog.* vol i: *Recorders, Fifes, and Simple System Transverse Flutes of One Key* (Washington, DC: Library of Congress, 1982).

TOFF, NANCY, *The Development of the Modern Flute* (New York: Taplinger, 1979).

—— *The Flute Book* (New York: Charles Scribner's Sons, 1985).

TOSI, PIER FRANCESCO, *Observations on the Florid Song* (Bologna, 1723); English trans. J. C. Galliard (1742; 2nd edn. 1743; repr., London: William Reeves, 1926, 1967; Stainer & Bell, 1987).

TRICHET, PIERRE, *Le traité des instruments de musique* (after 1638); ed. François Lesure, *Annales musicologiques*, 3 (1955), 332–49.

TROMLITZ, JOHANN GEORGE, *Ausfürlicher und gründlicher Unterricht die Flöte zu spielen* (Leipzig: Adam Friedrich Böhme, 1791); facsimile edn. (Buren: Frits Knuf, 1973); trans. and ed. Ardal Powell, with an introduction by Eileen Hadidian, as *The Virtuoso Flute-Player* (Cambridge: Cambridge University Press, 1991).

—— *Kurze Abhandlung vom Flötenspielen* (Leipzig: Breitkopf, 1786).

—— *Ueber die Flöten mit mehrern Klappen* (Leipzig: Adam Friedrich Böhme, 1800); facsimile edn. (Buren: Frits Knuf, 1973).

VANDERHAGEN, AMAND, *Nouvelle Méthode de Flute* (Paris: Pleyel, *c.*1799); facsimile edn. (Florence: Studio per Edizioni Scelte, 1984).

VESTER, FRANS, *Flute Music of the 18th Century* (Monteux: Musica Rara, 1985).

VIRDUNG, SEBASTIAN, *Musica getutscht* (Basle: Michael Furter, 1511); facsimile edn., ed. Klaus Wolfgang Niemöller (Kassel: Bärenreiter, 1970).

VIRGILIANO, AURELIO, *Il Dolcimelo*, MS bk. 3 (after 1600); facsimile edn., ed. Marcello Castellani (Florence: Studio per Edizioni Scelte, 1979).

WADE, RACHEL, W., *The Keyboard Concertos of Carl Philipp Emanuel Bach* (Ann Arbor, Mich.: UMI Research Press, 1981).

WARRACK, JOHN, *Carl Maria von Weber* (London: H. Hamilton, 1968; New York: Macmillan, 1968; 2nd edn., 1976).

WRAGG, J., *The Flute Preceptor* (London: The Author, 1792).
—— *Wragg's Improved Flute Preceptor*, (London: The Author, 1806).
YOUNG, PHILLIP T., *The Look of Music* (Seattle: University of Washington Press, 1980).
—— *Twenty-Five Hundred Historical Woodwind Instruments* (New York: Pendragon Press, 1982).
ZACCONI, LODOVICO, *Prattica di musica* (Venice: Girolamo Polo, 1592); facsimile edn. (Bologna: Forni Editore, [1967]).

Articles

ADDINGTON, CHRISTOPHER, 'In Search of the Baroque Flute: The Flute Family 1680–1750', *Early Music*, 12: 1 (1984), 34–47.
—— 'The Bach Flute', *Musical Quarterly*, 71: 3 (1985), 264–80.
BAINES, ANTHONY, 'Two Cassel Inventories', *Galpin Society Journal*, 4 (1951), 30–8.
BEST, TERENCE, 'Handel's Chamber Music: Sources, Chronology and Authenticity', *Early Music*, 13: 4 (1985), 476–99.
BINKLEY, THOMAS, 'A Perspective on Historical Performance', *Historical Performance*, 1: 1 (1988), 19–20.
BLOOM, PETER H., 'Observations on the Advantageous Use of the "Eight-Key" Flute', *Flutist Quarterly*, 11: 1 (1985), 18–25.
BOSSERT, GUSTAV, 'Die Hofkapelle unter Eberhard III., 1628–1657', *Württembergische Vierteljahrhefte für Landesgeschichte*, 21 (1912), 133–7.
BOWERS, JANE, '*Flaüste traverseinne* and *Flute d'Allemagne*—The Flute in France from the Late Middle Ages up through 1702' *Recherches sur la musique française classique*, 19 (1979), 7–49.
—— 'New Light on the Development of the Transverse Flute between about 1650 and about 1770', *Journal of the American Musical Instrument Society*, 3 (1977), 5–56.
BRÖHL, RICARDA, 'Die Flötensonaten Wolfgang Amadeus Mozarts', *Tibia*, 3 (1979), 369–77.
BROWN, HOWARD MAYER, 'Notes (and Transposing Notes) on the Transverse Flute in the Early Sixteenth Century', *Journal of the American Musical Instrument Society*, 12 (1986), 5–39.
—— 'Performing Practice', *The New Grove Dictionary of Music and Musicians*, xiv. 370–93, q.v.
—— 'The Flute', *The New Grove Dictionary of Music and Musicians*, vi. 664–81, q.v.
CASTELLANI, MARCELLO, 'Two Late-Renaissnace Transverse Flutes', *Galpin Society Journal*, 25 (1972), 73–9.
ELIASON, ROBERT E., 'George Catlin, Hartford Musical Instrument Maker', *Journal of the American Musical Instrument Society*, 8 and 9 (1982–3), 16–37, 21–52.
GODWIN, JOSCELYN, 'The Renaissance Flute', *The Consort*, 28 (1972), 70–81.
GREER, DEREK, 'The Flute Bands of Ireland', *Flutist Quarterly*, 11: 1 (1985), 41–3.

HALFPENNY, ERIC, 'A French Commentary on Quantz', *Music & Letters*, 37 (1956), 61–6.

HAYNES, BRUCE, 'Johann Sebastian Bach's Pitch Standards: The Woodwind Perspective', *Journal of the American Musical Instrument Society*, 11 (1985), 55–114.

—— 'Generic 415', *Traverso*, 1: 4 (1989), 1–2.

HETTRICK, WILLIAM E., 'Martin Agricola's Poetic Discussion of the Recorder and Other Woodwind Instruments', *American Recorder*, 21 (1980), 103–13; 23 (1982), 139–46; 24 (1985), 51–60.

HIBGEE, DALE, 'Baroque Flute Discography', *Early Music*, 7: 2 (1979), 250–3.

HORSLEY, IMOGENE, 'Improvised Embellishment in the Performance of Renaissance Polyphonic Music', *Journal of the American Musicological Society*, 4 (1951), 3–19.

—— 'The Solo Ricercar in Diminution Manuals: New Light on Early Wind and String Techniques', *Acta Musicologica*, 33 (1961), 29–40.

—— 'Wind Techniques in the Sixteenth and Early Seventeenth Centuries', *Brass Quarterly*, 4 (1960), 49–63.

KAMMERER, RAFAEL, 'William Kincaid: Sights Set on a New Horizon', *Musical America* (Aug. 1960), 27–8.

KRUEGER, CHRISTOPHER, 'Playing Baroque Music on the Modern Flute', *Flutist Quarterly*, 13: 1 (1988), 44–53.

LASOCKI, DAVID, and BEST, TERENCE, 'A New Flute Sonata by Handel', *Early Music*, 9: 3 (1981), 307–11; rev. version in *Flutist Quarterly*, 10: 3 (1985), 29–31, 34–5.

LAWRENCE, ELEANOR, 'Interview with Shelley Gruskin', *Newsletter of the National Flute Association*, 6: 3 (1981), 3, 10–13, 18.

LEQUIN, FRANK, 'Mozarts " . . . rarer Mann"', *Mitteilungen der Internationalen Stiftung Mozarteum*, 29: double vol. 1–2 (1981), 3–19.

LINDO, DEREK, 'The Renaissance Military Flute', *Renaissance Flute Circle Newsletter*, 1 (1988), 3–5.

MARSHALL, ROBERT L., 'J. S. Bach's Compositions for Solo Flute: A Reconsideration of Their Authenticity and Chronology', *Journal of the American Musicological Society*, 32: 3 (1979), 463–98; repr. in Marshall, *The Music of Johann Sebastian Bach: The Sources, the Style, the Significance* (New York: Schirmer Books, 1989), 201–25.

MARX, JOSEF, 'The Tone of the Baroque Oboe', *Galpin Society Journal*, 4 (1951), 3–19.

MENDEL, ARTHUR, 'On the Pitches in Use in Bach's Time', *Musical Quarterly*, 41 (1955), 332–54, 466–80.

—— 'Pitch in the 16th and Early 17th Centuries', *Musical Quarterly*, 34 (1948), 28–45, 199–221, 336–57, 575–93.

—— 'Pitch in Western Music Since 1500: A Re-examination', *Acta Musicologica*, 50 (1978), 1–93, 328.

O'DONNELL, JOHN, 'The French Style and the Overtures of Bach', *Early Music*, 7: 2 and 3 (1979), 191–6, 336–45.

POOR, MARY LOUISE, 'Problems of Transference from Boehm to Baroque Flute', *Newsletter of the National Flute Association*, 6: 3 (1981), 6–7.

PUGLISI, FILADELFIO, 'A Survey of Renaissance Flutes', *Galpin Society Journal*, 41 (1988), 67–82.

REILLY, EDWARD R., 'Further Musical Examples for Quantz's *Versuch*', *Journal of the American Musicological Society*, 17: 2 (1964), 157–69.

SMITH, ANNE, 'Belege zur Frage der Stimmtonhöhe bei Michael Praetorius', in Peter Reidemeister and Veronika Gutmann, eds., *Alte Musik: Praxis und Reflexion* (Winterthur: Amadeus Verlag, 1983).

—— 'Die Renaissancequerflöte und ihre Musik, ein Beitrag zur Interpretation der Quellen', *Basler Jahrbuch für historische Musikpraxis*, 2 (1978), 9–76.

SMITH, CARLETON SPRAGUE, 'Haydn's Chamber Music and the Flute', *Musical Quarterly*, 19: 3 and 4 (1933), 341–50, 434–55.

SOLUM, JOHN, 'On Perceiving the Written-Out Ornaments in Movements from Bach's Flute Sonatas', *Flutist Quarterly*, 10: 3 (1985), 26–7.

—— review of Margaret N. Neuhaus, *The Baroque Flute Fingering Book, Newsletter* of the American Musical Instrument Society, 16: 2 (June 1987), 13.

—— review of Betty Bang Mather, *Interpretation of French Music from 1675 to 1775*, *Pro Musica*, 1: 6 (1976), 10–11.

—— review of Betty Bang Mather and David Lasocki, *Free Ornamentation in Woodwind Music 1700–1775*, *The Consort*, 34 (1978), 315.

TYSON, ALAN, 'Haydn and Two Stolen Trios', *Music Review*, 22 (1961), 21–7.

VAN ACHT, ROB, 'Dutch Wind-Instrument Makers from 1670 to 1820', *Galpin Society Journal*, 41 (1988), 83–101.

VAN DER STRAETEN, EDMOND, *La Musique aux Pay-Bas* (Brussels: C. A. van Trigt, 1885), vii. 439–44, viii, 306–7.

WATERHOUSE, WILLIAM, 'A Newly Discovered 17th-Century Bassoon by Haka', *Early Music*, 16: 3 (1988), 407–10.

WEBER, RAINER, 'Some Researches into Pitch in the 16th Century with Particular Reference to the Instruments in the Accademia Filarmonica of Verona', *Galpin Society Journal*, 28 (1975), 7–10.

WOLFF, CHRISTOPH, 'Bach's Leipzig Chamber Music', *Early Music*, 13: 2 (1985), 165–75.

YOUNG, PHILLIP T., 'The Scherers of Butzbach', *Galpin Society Journal*, 39 (1986), 112–24.

ZASLAW, NEAL, 'Toward the Revival of the Classical Orchestra', *Proceedings of the Royal Musical Association*, 103 (1976–7), 158–87.

Index

Note: Page numbers in *italic* type refer to illustrations; those in **bold** type indicate both text and illustration references.

Index compiled by Frank Pert